How can I be sure?

How can I be sure?

by

Frank Allred

GRACE PUBLICATIONS TRUST
175 Tower Bridge Road
LONDON SE1 2AH
England

Joint Managing Editors
J.P.Arthur MA
H.J.Appleby

First published 1999

ISBN 0946462 577

Distributed by:
EVANGELICAL PRESS
Faverdale North Industrial Estate
DARLINGTON
DL3 OPH
England

Printed in Great Britain by: Cox & Wyman, Reading

Cover design by: Colin Fairchild

Contents

Preface

My purpose in writing this little book is to help my Christian brothers and sisters to be more aware of their privileges and so to encourage them to feel more secure as the redeemed children of God. By 'Christians' I mean people who freely acknowledge their transgressions; who trust in Jesus Christ alone for salvation; who are experiencing something of the transforming power of the Holy Spirit; and who believe the Bible to be the Word of God. I do not have in mind those who call themselves Christians but deny the Faith in any of its principal parts, or those whose Christianity is merely a formality.

Spiritual insecurity among Christians is widespread today and is due mainly to a loss of confidence in the gospel. Many are simply not sure about what they believe and, for this reason, they hesitate in their witness, are half-hearted in their Christian service and, in some cases, are even uncertain about how Christians should behave.

Claiming to be sure about what we believe is not popular today. It leaves the believer open to the charge of gullibility by those who think they know better, and to the charge of arrogance by those who think it is a virtue to glorify doubt. The authority of the Bible, on which our security rests, is no longer assumed. Belief in the divine origin of the Scriptures is regarded, not as an essential element in knowing God, but rather as a barrier to it. In such an atmosphere, Christians who lack assurance are bound to feel threatened.

However, after many years in the ministry of the church, I am persuaded that the real reason for the prevailing lack of assurance is not the scepticism about the Bible on the part of those who do not believe, but the ignorance of it on the part of those who do. Whatever unbelievers may say, God has not gone back on his Word, and when insecure Christians begin to be more diligent in their study of it, their confidence will grow.

Obviously, the uncertainty of individual church members is

bound to weaken the witness of the whole church. Unless confidence in God's Word is restored and ignorance of it dispelled, the influence of the church will go on declining. People will continue to see her as irrelevant. Why should they do otherwise?

Introduction

If I want to be sure of going to heaven, I must be able to say an emphatic 'yes' to two questions. The first is: 'Is the Lord Jesus Christ trustworthy?' The second: 'Will he bring *me* safely to heaven?' The questions must be answered in this order because if I cannot say 'yes' to the first, it is obvious I cannot say 'yes' to the second.

We may, of course, frame the first question in many different ways: 'Is the Lord Jesus Christ all he claims to be?' 'Will he keep his promises?' 'Is he the only one who can forgive sins?' 'Is he the only one who has the words of eternal life?' Likewise the second: 'Is he everything to *me*?' 'Do his promises apply to *me*?' 'Has he forgiven *my* sins?' 'Has he given *me* the gift of eternal life?'

During the course of church history, both questions have been keenly debated. From the Reformation in the sixteenth century until the authority of the Bible was challenged in the eighteenth, the question as to whether it is possible for believers to know they have eternal life was studied at greater depth than it has been, before or since. But even among those who were persuaded that assurance of salvation is attainable, deep disagreements emerged.

John Calvin and the early Reformers gave the impression that whoever lacked assurance did not possess true faith, because faith itself is the sure knowledge of God's favour towards us. At face value this means that anyone who does not enjoy complete assurance cannot have genuine faith (although Calvin also taught that no believer is ever *entirely* free of doubts). The Reformers were, of course, eager to stress the importance of personal assurance because they were reacting against the teaching of the Roman Catholic Church which flatly rejected the idea of a believer being sure. Rome taught that such assurance was given only by special revelation to a favoured few — like Stephen and Paul — and to no-one else. It was in the interests of the Church of Rome to adopt this position, because if a believer was sure of his or her eternal salvation in Christ, the Church could no longer hold him or her captive. Absolution from a priest would no longer be needed.

Differences of a different kind emerged later. The Puritans of the seventeenth century taught that a person may have genuine faith but 'may wait long, and conflict with many difficulties' before finally reaching the point of being sure of salvation. The impression was given (although it may not have been intended) that assurance is something *added* to faith. Inevitably, this led the insecure believer, in the desire for assurance, into long periods of heart-searching and self-examination.

In sharp contrast John Wesley, in the eighteenth century, taught that conversion carries an immediate certainty with it. When sinners become aware of their sins and turn to Christ in repentance, the Holy Spirit gives a direct and immediate assurance without which their conversion could not be regarded as genuine. There being no need for self-examination, believers are therefore able to rejoice at once in the assurance that they are the redeemed children of God.

So who is right — the Reformers, the Puritans or the Wesleyans? In fairness to the Reformers, some of their writings clearly teach that doubts may be present in the heart of a true believer. Although faith is being sure of eternal salvation, the presence of doubts may weaken that assurance.

The problem with the Wesleyan view is that John Wesley also taught that it is possible for the believer to fall away and be lost. It is the responsibility of Christians to keep themselves in a state of grace. The question arises: How can believers know they are secure if there is the ever-present possibility that they may lose their salvation and be lost? If believers are not standing on solid ground, how can they get rid of the feeling that they may sink at any moment? In these circumstances, assurance becomes almost meaningless. And in any case, why would the Holy Spirit convey a sense of assurance to the believer's heart if there is no certainty of *eternal* security? God cannot be guilty of deception.

The Puritan teaching also has its dangers if it is not properly understood. Self-examination does, of course, have an important place. The Christians in Corinth were urged to examine themselves to make sure they were 'in the faith' (2 Cor.13:5). But those who have a tendency to be always looking inward, searching their hearts to find some evidence that they are truly God's children, easily open themselves to yet further anxiety and uncertainty. Christians of this temperament should realise that confidence grows as we look to Jesus. Assurance deepens in an atmosphere of active obedience and in a climate of worship, fellowship, service, Bible-study and prayer.

Although we may learn a lot from the arguments of the past, Scripture is our only reliable guide, and Scripture clearly defines faith as 'being sure of what we hope for' (Heb.11:1) and yet provides many examples of true believers whose faith was weak because they were afflicted with doubts. So yes! It is possible to have genuine faith and still lack assurance. The experience of countless numbers of Christian people confirms this view. But Scripture also urges us to be eager to reach the point where we know for sure that we are God's children — for ever.

Sadly, in the later nineteenth and twentieth centuries, the subject has been virtually sidelined; its importance is now barely recognised in the church. To some extent this is due to the fact that the dispute over the inspiration and authority of Scripture has raised more fundamental questions. Obviously, when doubts about the trustworthiness of Christ are entertained, the matter of personal assurance is precluded. But the sad result is that in today's church, very many believers remain unaware of one of the Holy Spirit's most precious gifts — the assurance of eternal life. It is a most serious loss.

Readers may also like to know of the title *The roots of true faith* (ISBN 0-946462-28-3) which is also published by Grace Publications, dealing with subjects related to the matter of Christian assurance.

Key points of chapter one — the problem of insecurity

- a common condition
- some misunderstandings
- insecurity temporal
- are faith and assurance the same?

1.
The problem of insecurity

A common condition

The Bible tells us that God wants his children to be sure about two things ¾ about going to heaven and about his care over them until they get there. Having assurance means being sure of these two things. It means being fully persuaded that God will do for us, his children, exactly what he has promised in the Bible. It means knowing that we have an inheritance in heaven which we shall share with the Lord Jesus Christ (Romans 8:17) who has gone to prepare a place for us (John 14:2). It means knowing that in all our experiences in this life, God is working for our eternal good (Romans 8:28).

The apostle Paul sums up his own assurance in this way ¾ 'I know whom I have believed, and am convinced that he is able to guard what I have entrusted to him...' (2 Timothy 1:12); 'I am convinced that neither death nor life, neither angels nor demons, neither the present nor the future, nor any powers, neither height nor depth, nor anything else in all creation, will be able to separate us from the love of God that is in Christ Jesus our Lord' (Romans 8:38, 39).

The Bible tells us how we can feel sure. The apostle John wrote his first letter for this very purpose. 'I write these things,' he says, 'to you who believe in the name of the Son of God so that you may know that you have eternal life' (1 John 5:13).

God has given us many precious promises on which to base our assurance. Take for example, the words of Jesus, 'My sheep listen to my voice; I know them, and they follow me. I give them eternal life, and they shall never perish; no-one can snatch them out of my hand' (John 10:28). Or take the words of the apostle Paul '... he who began a good work in you will carry it on to completion until the day of Christ Jesus' (Philippians 1:6).

Having assurance makes the Christian life more relevant and fulfilling. It transforms our outlook; puts the things of this world in their proper perspective, and helps us face life's hardships with calmness and fortitude. Assurance is a feeling of certainty, and yet much more than a feeling. Although our emotions are deeply affected by it, spiritual certainty is rooted in our understanding of what God has done for us in Christ. It means knowing, in our hearts and minds, the hope to which he has called us (Ephesians 1:18).

In spite of all this, insecurity among believers is common. Many Christians simply do not know they can be sure. They are not aware that God has, in his great mercy, provided everything they need to be sure. This is a serious problem, not least because believers cannot be at their best for God in this life if they are uncertain about going to be with Christ in the next (Philippians 1:21-24). They simply cannot live the Christian life to the full. The quality of their service for the Master, the choices they make, the effectiveness of their prayers, and not least, their enjoyment of God will all be adversely affected. The good news is, they need not remain in this condition.

Some misunderstandings

Many people don't like Christians to talk about being sure. Usually, this is because these objectors believe heaven is a reward for doing good and they insist that no-one can know

15

whether he is good enough to go to heaven until the Day of Judgment. Therefore, they say, all who claim to be sure must have a high opinion of themselves. But this is a serious mistake. It rests on a complete misunderstanding of the gospel. Being sure does not depend on what we do for God, but on what he has done for us. We cannot enjoy the blessings of assurance unless and until we have the humility to admit that we are not, and never will be, good enough to go to heaven.

Others think that Christians who say they are sure must be naïve. A bishop of the Church of England once told me that no-one could be as confident as I claimed to be without having a 'closed mind'. His comments were made after he and I, together with other ministers, had been talking about some aspects of the Christian Faith. I had only just been ordained and felt it would not have been good manners to argue with the bishop. But later I was very sorry I did not answer him. I have wondered many times since what he would have said about the long list of men and women mentioned in Hebrews chapter eleven who were commended for having a faith which the writer describes as 'being sure of what we hope for and certain of what we do not see' (Hebrews 11:1). Did all these great men and women of faith have 'closed minds'? I think not.

Others think believers can never be sure because, they say, scholars have proved that we can no longer rely on what the Bible says. They are really saying that if we are sure, it is because we are ignorant of what scholars have discovered. But assurance is God's gift to all who sincerely believe his promises; and those who believe know that God's Word *can* be trusted. God has taught them to rely on his Word, not by keeping them in ignorance, but by opening their minds and hearts to its truth and by their proving its power in their lives. The Scriptures have made them 'wise for salvation through faith in Christ Jesus' (2 Timothy 3:15). Those who refuse to believe, no matter how much knowledge *about* the Bible they may have, cannot have this testimony in their hearts. It is impossible.

16

Yet others think that we who want to be sure about going to heaven are selfish. How dare we spend time studying the Scriptures to be sure of our own salvation when the world is falling apart around us? Are we not guilty, like the infamous Roman emperor Nero, of fiddling while Rome burns? But what these critics fail to understand is that Christians who are convinced about their faith are usually much better equipped to deal with today's moral and spiritual problems than those who are not. Indeed, many problems would not have arisen at all if Christians had been more confident about their faith. People who deny the Christian Faith and reject Christian morality are influential only because so many Christians, who should be fighting for the Faith, are not sure of it in their own experience.

Insecurity is temporal

Although Christians who lack assurance miss the best, their loss is not permanent. God's children cannot take their doubts to heaven. When we die, all our doubts will die as well. 'When perfection comes,' says Paul, '... I shall know fully, even as I am fully known' (1 Corinthians 13:12). If eternal life were only for those who never had any doubts, none of us would go to heaven. Having eternal life depends on God's decree and not on our being sure. Whether we are sure or not, there cannot be the slightest doubt about the salvation of those whom God has called and who have been born of the Spirit. The apostle Peter says, 'Praise be to the God and Father of our Lord Jesus Christ! In his great mercy he has given us new birth into a living hope through the resurrection of Jesus Christ from the dead, and into an inheritance that can never perish, spoil or fade ¾ kept in heaven for you, who through faith are shielded by God's power until the coming of the salvation that is ready to be revealed in the last time' (1 Peter 1:3-5).

17

How can I be sure?

We know how we can go into a restaurant and choose an empty table, pleasantly situated in a corner, only to find a card on the table which says 'Reserved'. That tells us that the management is keeping that table for customers who have not yet arrived. So it is with God. He has prepared a place for us (John 14:2, 3) and one day he will receive us into his presence. And not only that, he is also shielding us by his power during our journey, and will make sure we arrive safely (1 Peter 1:5). Heaven is a reserved place for a preserved people.

To put it another way, being secure does not depend on the strength of our faith but on the One on whom our faith rests. The believer with the weakest faith is as safe as the believer with the strongest. If our salvation depended on how much faith we had, we would *never* feel secure because we would never know whether or not we had enough. But God saves all who truly believe whether they feel sure about it or not. Their salvation does not depend on the way they feel but on his eternal purpose (Ephesians 1:4).

Some people do not believe this. They say the Bible teaches that it is possible for Christians to fall away and be lost. Does Paul not talk about those who have 'shipwrecked their faith' (1 Timothy 1:19) and Peter about those who deny 'the sovereign Lord who bought them'? (2 Peter 2:1). But when we look at these texts more closely, we see that the faith of such people was not genuine from the start. They were false teachers, not true Christians. The apostle John tells us that there were people in the early church who claimed to be Christians, but they left because they never really belonged in the first place. 'For if they had belonged to us' he explains, 'they would have remained with us; but their going showed that none of them belonged to us' (1 John 2:19). It is just the same today. Many people are Christians in name only. Their names may be on the membership roll of the church on earth, but they are not written in the book of life (Revelation 13:8).

18

But, it is argued, there are many warnings in the Bible about 'falling away'. If true believers cannot be lost, why are believers urged to continue in their faith (Colossians 1: 23) or warned to 'pay more careful attention to what we have heard, so that we do not drift away'? (Hebrews 2:1). It all seems so unnecessary. But before we jump to conclusions, we must ask ourselves, Would God reveal to us that we were chosen in Christ 'before the creation of the world' and 'predestined to be adopted as his sons' (Ephesians 1:4, 5) and *then* tell us that we may be lost forever? God does not contradict himself. What he gives with one hand he does not take away with the other.

The warnings are necessary because people may deceive themselves. They may think they are Christians, and in many ways look like Christians, but in reality they are still strangers to the grace of God. This is why the subject of assurance is so important. And this is why the Bible insists on obedience to God's Word, love for others, and correct belief, as evidences of true faith. The person who believes what he likes, does as he pleases, and still insists that he is going to heaven, is deceiving himself.

For God's true children, the warnings are all part of the help God gives us to make sure we persevere to the end. Warnings make us keenly aware of the sins which lead to destruction and help us to be very careful to avoid them. To suggest that the warnings are intended to make us doubt God's precious promises is absurd, for through those promises we 'participate in the divine nature and escape the corruption in the world' (2 Peter 1:4).

Some verses in Hebrews chapter six may seem, at first sight, to teach that it is possible to fall away. Indeed, many Christians have been disturbed by them. Here again, close examination is necessary. The writer says, 'It is impossible for those who have once been enlightened, who have tasted the heavenly gift, who have shared in the Holy Spirit, who have tasted the goodness of the word of God and the powers of the coming age, if they

19

fall away, to be brought back to repentance ...' (Hebrews 6:4-6). Surely such people must be Christians, and if so, it must be possible to be saved and then lost again. But when we look a little closer, we discover that a person may experience all these things without being truly saved. The writer actually tells his readers he is confident of 'better things' in *their* case, 'things that accompany salvation' and he goes on to explain what these better things are: 'God is not unjust; he will not forget your work and the love you have shown him as you have helped his people and continue to help them' (Hebrews 6:9, 10). This love for God and his people is something more than being enlightened in the ways the writer mentions. It is evidence of the new birth. It is, of course, a very serious matter for those who have been enlightened not to do anything about living by that enlightenment, but the point is clear, they are not saved until they do.

The parable of the sower makes the same point. Some receive the Word of God into their hearts, but like the seed sown along the path where the ground is hard, they do not understand. Some, like the seed sown on rocky places where there is no depth of soil, receive the Word with joy, but quickly fall away. Others, like the seed sown among the thorns, begin to show signs of life and growth, but the worries of this life and the deceitfulness of wealth make it unfruitful (Matthew 13:1-9, 16-23). Being fruitful means producing the fruit of the Spirit ¾ 'love, joy, peace, patience, kindness, goodness, faithfulness, gentleness and self-control' (Galatians 5:22). This is the evidence of genuine faith.

Are faith and assurance the same thing?

The writer to the Hebrews says, 'Faith is being sure of what we hope for and certain of what we do not see' (Hebrews 11:1). This seems to suggest that a person who is not sure cannot have genuine faith and therefore faith and assurance must be the same thing. The apostle Peter, on the other hand, seems to say that assurance and faith are not the same thing. He says we are to 'make every effort' to add Christian virtues to our faith so that we may 'make our calling and election sure' (2 Peter 1: 5-11). How do we reconcile these two statements?

I have a friend who claims he has never had a single doubt about his salvation since the day he became a Christian. He insists that if a person doubts, however slightly, his faith cannot be genuine. For him, faith and assurance are indeed the same thing. By contrast, I have doubts but do not feel at all threatened by them. They slip into my mind without warning and usually go away within a second or two. Of course, I am indignant against myself when this happens. But I am even more indignant against my friend because he is implying that my faith cannot be real just because I have occasional fleeting doubts. (To be frank, I can't help feeling that he stubbornly refuses to admit his doubts, even to himself, because to do so would make him feel insecure.) Now which of us is right? Does the Bible teach that if I have faith then I must also feel sure of my salvation? Or does it teach that I can have genuine faith and yet feel insecure? As we have just seen, at first sight, it seems to teach both.

As soon as we understand that faith varies in strength, the problem becomes less acute. Our faith may be strong (i.e. few doubts), or it may be weak (i.e. many doubts). The writer to the Hebrews is talking about faith; not about faith mixed with doubt, and it is obvious that if I did not have any doubts I would have complete assurance. So when he says faith is 'being sure', he is not suggesting that those whose faith is not perfect cannot know anything about assurance. If this were the case, he would be contradicting himself because in chapter six he urges his readers to show diligence in order to make their hope sure (Hebrews 6:11).

The Bible makes it very clear that faith may be weak, and that it should grow stronger. Many examples of weak but

21

genuine and increasing faith have been recorded for our encouragement. The disciple Peter's faith was not strong enough to keep him from sinking when Jesus invited him to walk on the water (Matthew 14:28-31). The sick boy's father said to Jesus, 'I do believe, help me overcome my unbelief' (Mark 9:24). Paul gave thanks to God because the faith of the Christians in Thessalonica was 'growing more and more ...' (2 Thessalonians 1:3).

The proof of true faith is obedience, which surely means that the evidence of increasing faith is increasing obedience. With increasing obedience comes increasing assurance. We shall come back to this later.

It is possible of course, to believe God's Word and do nothing about it. This is why the apostle James warns us that 'faith without deeds is dead' (James 2:26). 'Show me your faith without deeds,' he says, 'and I will show you my faith by what I do. You believe that there is one God. Good! Even the demons believe that ¾ and shudder' (James 2:18,19).

Key points of chapter two — the symptoms of insecurity

- fear of death
- fear of life
- fear of man
- lost sense of vocation
- little interest in the Bible
- worldliness

2.
The symptoms of insecurity

The fear of death

I went to visit a man whose wife had become a Christian. Since her conversion, he had been treating her unkindly. He ridiculed her belief in God and poured scorn on the gospel. During our conversation I asked him if he was afraid to die. Picking up a safety pin, which was the nearest thing to hand, and holding it rather menacingly in front of my face, he said, angrily,
'Do you see *that*?'
'Yes, of course,' I answered.
'When I am dead,' he asserted, emphasizing every word, 'I shall be as dead as *that* ... forever! Why should I be afraid?'
I did not see much point in continuing the conversation. It was my impression that this man's confidence (if he really believed what he was saying) was based on wilful ignorance. Evidently he had succeeded in persuading himself that death was the end of everything, and as far as he was concerned, that was also the end of the matter.

Like the ostrich, it is possible to bury one's head in the sand and think the danger from the hunter has passed. But such security is false. The danger has not gone away; it has only increased. Conquest of the fear of death depends, not on obstinate ignorance about its serious consequences, but on the sure knowledge that Christ has conquered death for all who believe. Christians need not be afraid of opening their minds to face the challenge of death fearlessly, because they will never find a reason to be afraid of it.

Yet many Christians are afraid of death, and there are various causes. It may be because we are not yet sure that we are 'in Christ Jesus' and therefore free from condemnation (Romans 8:1). It may be because we still doubt God's ability to keep us from falling away. Or it may be because we have not yet understood the gospel properly.

Whatever the cause, the cure for this depressing condition lies in a deeper understanding of what God has done for us; a clearer realisation that we are 'justified freely by his grace through the redemption that came by Christ Jesus' (Romans 3:24). Our sins are reckoned as his and his righteousness is reckoned as ours. Once God has pronounced us 'not guilty' he will never again count our sins against us because our legal position before him has changed forever. No charge can ever be brought against us because God's verdict is final (Romans 8:33). The sting of death has been drawn (1 Corinthians 15:55-57). 'There is now no condemnation for those who are in Christ Jesus' (Romans 8:1). And because nothing can separate us from the love of Christ (Romans 8:35-39), we may look forward with confidence to the perfect enjoyment of his presence.

The writer to the Hebrews tells us that Jesus shared in our humanity 'so that by death he might destroy him who holds the power of death — that is, the devil — and free those who all their lives were held in slavery by their fear of death' (Hebrews 2:14, 15). The devil has the power of death only by God's permission — like a prison governor who has been given power over his prisoners by the state, and must release them as soon as he receives orders to do so from higher authority. The devil no longer has the power of death over believers because Christ has paid the penalty for their sins and set them free.

How can I be sure?

The apostle Paul actually *looked forward* to death! He didn't know which to choose — to go to be with Christ or to go on serving him in this world. If his personal desire to be with the Lord had not been softened by the needs of the Christians he had been called to serve, he would have died happily. 'What shall I do?' he asks. 'I do not know! I am torn between the two: I desire to depart and be with Christ, which is better by far, but it is more necessary for you that I remain in the body' (Philippians 1:22, 23).

'Ah but ...' we say, 'it was easier for Paul. He didn't have a wife and family to leave behind, and he suffered so much in this world he was much more likely to be happy to leave it than we are. In any case, he had special revelations from God.' But if we say this about Paul, what do we say about the countless numbers of Christians since his day, who had wives, families, comforts, and *no* special revelations, and yet they conquered the fear of death and looked forward to being with Christ, with the same calm assurance as Paul?

Of course, there is a world of difference between the fear of death and the fear of dying. No-one likes the thought of dying. We shrink with horror from the prospect of a slow and painful death. Many believers have suffered great distress during their last illness, their spirits brought low by prolonged suffering, the loss of their faculties, or the effect of drugs. Those of us who have been close to the deaths of a significant number of God's children know that it is not true to say that convinced Christians always die joyfully.

I remember two ladies, both of whom had been faithful servants of Christ. On her death bed, one of them was looking forward so much to being with the Lord that she arranged her own funeral service without the slightest anxiety. The only thing that bothered her was whether her husband would have his regular bath after she had gone! The other lady died feeling very depressed because she felt that her service for the Master had not been of the highest standard. Her life had, in fact, been a shining example to others, but she, judging herself harshly, did not think so. As she came near the end, the problem seemed to become more acute. Both women were sure of their destiny, but in the hour of death one was looking forward and the other looking back. I suppose it may have had something to do with their different temperaments.

To come back to the point, it is the fear of what death itself may bring which is a symptom of our insecurity — the fear of punishment; the fear of being excluded from the presence of God. If this fear still lingers in our hearts, it can only mean that we are not yet fully persuaded that Christ has robbed death of all its terrors for all his people; that 'death has been swallowed up in victory' (1 Corinthians 15:54).

The words of Jesus should be enough to remove all our doubts. 'I tell you the truth, whoever hears my word and believes him who sent me, has eternal life and will not be condemned; he has crossed over from death to life' (John 5:24).

The fear of life

The fear of death and the fear of life often survive together in the same Christian heart. A believer who is not sure about God's promise of eternal life is not likely to be sure about God's preservation in this life. Yet both are promised to all God's children. We have 'an inheritance in heaven which cannot perish, spoil or fade' and we are 'shielded by God's power' so that we cannot fail to enter it (1 Peter 1: 4,5). Those whom God saves, he keeps.

Does this give us immunity from trials? Not at all. It gives us something better — the assurance that all our trials are in the plan and purpose of God and for our benefit (1 Thessalonians 3:3). 'We know,' says the apostle Paul, 'that in all things God works for the good of those who love him, who have been called according to his purpose' (Romans 8:28). When Paul wrote these words he was thinking particularly about

27

the present sufferings of believers, and he is teaching us that God actually uses them for our good — not necessarily our temporal good (i.e. good health and success in this world) — but our eternal good.

As God's children 'we live by faith and not by sight' (2 Corinthians 5:7). We must not form our opinion of God's ability to keep his promises by what we see around us. If we do, we shall run into all sorts of trouble, for his paths are 'beyond tracing out!' (Romans 11:33). When things go wrong (as we say), we shall begin to wonder if God has forgotten us. We simply cannot judge by appearances. Look at Abraham for example. When God promised him a child in his old age, things didn't look at all promising. But 'without weakening in his faith, he faced the fact that his body was as good as dead — since he was about a hundred years old — and that Sarah's womb was also dead. Yet he did not waver through unbelief regarding the promise of God, but was strengthened in his faith and gave glory to God, being fully persuaded that God had power to do what he had promised' (Romans 4:19-21).

Being sure of God's providential care then, doesn't mean being able to understand his ways. It means putting our trust in his Word without trying to explain why he allows this or that to happen. 'Who has understood the Spirit of the Lord, or instructed him as his counsellor?' 'His understanding no-one can fathom' (Isaiah 40: 13, 28).

If we do not trust in the Lord to keep us, we lose our first defence against anxiety. Our troubles are aggravated because we are not sure there is a purpose in them. Our peace of mind is disturbed because we fear things might get out of control. And we slip, all too easily, into that superstitious frame of mind so common among unbelievers, which expresses itself by crossing fingers and touching wood.

'The LORD watches over you,' said the Psalmist, '... he will keep you from all harm — he will watch over your life; the LORD will watch over your coming and going both now and for evermore' (Psalm 121:5-8). With such a promise, why should we be afraid of life?

The fear of unbelievers

'Do not be frightened,' says the apostle Peter, '... always be prepared to give an answer to everyone who asks you to give the reason for the hope that you have' (1 Peter 3:14, 15). But if we are not sure about the hope that we have, we can hardly be prepared to give the reason for it. It takes courage to stand for Christ in the world and no-one can find the courage to say why he is a Christian if he is not sure that he is. We must have our convictions before we can have the courage of our convictions.

Thankfully, in most countries, no-one can put us in prison or put us to death just because we are Christians, but even so there are *other* more subtle ways of persecution. Every Christian must face the fact that 'the message of the cross is foolishness to those who are perishing' (1 Corinthians 1:18). Unbelievers usually regard the teaching that salvation can only come through a Jew, crucified two thousand years ago, as ridiculous. They don't take kindly to the Bible's teaching about sin and repentance, either. In these circumstances, Christians who are not sure about their faith will be fearful or embarrassed or both, when they are challenged about it, and the temptation to dilute the message will always be present.

Uncertainty and fear usually go hand-in-hand. When Jesus was arrested, one of the reasons why his disciples 'deserted him and fled' (Matthew 26:56) was because they did not understand what was going on. The huge gaps in their knowledge about the purpose of their Lord's approaching death left them confused and fearful. Peter had imagined he had the courage to die with Christ, but when the test came, he failed (John 13:36-38). Under test, he was so paralysed by fear that he denied his Lord with an oath (Matthew 26:71, 72).

Conviction and courage also go hand-in-hand. What a difference Pentecost made in the lives of the apostles! Their grasp of the gospel truth and their boldness were so impressive, even the persecuting authorities were astonished (Acts 4:13). Even before the day of Pentecost, Jesus had 'opened their minds so they could understand the Scriptures' (Luke 24:45); and now the Spirit gave them power to preach what had been revealed to them, fearlessly and effectively (Acts 1:8). To think of the apostles receiving power without enlightenment or enlightenment without power is absurd. And what was true of them is also true of us. The Spirit does not open our minds to the truth so that we can keep it to ourselves. Nor does he give us boldness to speak if we are not sure what to say.

The link between knowing and speaking the truth without fear is evident in the writings of the apostles. 'If you suffer as a Christian', says Peter, 'do not be ashamed, but praise God that you bear that name' (1 Peter 4:16). 'I am not ashamed of the gospel of Christ,' says Paul, 'because it is the power of God for the salvation of everyone who believes' (Romans 1:16). 'I eagerly expect and hope that I will in no way be ashamed, but will have sufficient courage so that now as always Christ will be exalted in my body, whether by life or by death. For to me, to live is Christ and to die is gain' (Philippians 1:19-21).

This opening of the mind is, of course, more than an improvement in our Christian education. It is an enlightening of 'the eyes of your heart' (Ephesians 1:18). Mere head-knowledge does nothing to remove the fear of men. When the Spirit gives understanding, our entire being is affected, so that we have no further need to be afraid of anyone. As the Spirit reveals God's truth to us, he also assures us of his protection in our earthly pilgrimage (as we have seen) and of the security of our eternal inheritance. He persuades us that God will keep his promises to guard us 'as the apple of his eye' (Deuteronomy 32:10).

'In God I trust; I will not be afraid', said the psalmist, 'What can mortal man do to me?' (Psalm 56:4). The answer is — only what our wise and loving heavenly Father allows him to do. But if we do not have the psalmist's trust, we shall find it hard to conquer the fear of men.

A lost sense of vocation

Another strong link — between knowing and serving — is also clearly seen in the New Testament. After writing at some length in the earlier chapters of his letter to the Romans about the secure position of those who are in Christ and about their future glory, Paul goes on to show what this means in terms of Christian service. He says, 'I urge you, brothers, in view of God's mercy, to offer your bodies as living sacrifices, holy and pleasing to God — which is your spiritual worship' (Romans 12:1). Similarly, when writing to the Christians in Corinth, Paul makes a moving appeal— 'Therefore, my dear brothers, stand firm. Let nothing move you. Always give yourselves fully to the work of the Lord, because you know that your labour in the Lord is not in vain' (1 Corinthians 15:58). On what basis does he make this appeal? Christ has been raised from the dead and we too will be raised, imperishable! The same connection is made yet again when Paul writes to Christian slaves. 'Whatever you do, work at it with all your heart, as working for the Lord, not for men, since you know that you will receive an inheritance from the Lord as a reward. It is the Lord Christ you are serving' (Colossians 3:23, 24).

The reason for this link between knowing and serving is obvious. Being sure Christ has secured our eternal inheritance fills our hearts with gratitude so that we have a strong desire to serve our God faithfully. We want our lives to be one long thanksgiving to him.

How can I be sure?

Some try to deny this and say that assurance leads to slackness. Far better they say, for God to leave us uncertain about our destiny so that we shall work all the harder. Obviously, people of this opinion have no assurance and are therefore not in a position to make the criticism. Christians who have assurance know from their own experience what a powerful incentive it is to Christian service.

Lack of assurance on the other hand, leads to the loss of a sense of vocation. Behind a shaky devotion there is usually a shaky faith. For if we are not sure about our inheritance in the next life, we cannot be sure about our priorities in this. Insecure Christians are seldom found seeking the Lord's will for their lives. They are much more likely to be found trying to serve both God and money (Matthew 6:24).

Proof of this is not hard to find. The church is handicapped by dubious believers who completely fail to consider what their Christian calling might be. In their secular jobs they are not aware of their responsibility as the servants of Christ. They are 'Sunday Christians', and even then it is usually only when it is convenient for them. Their minds are given over to worldly pursuits and they rarely recognize any opportunities to speak a word for Christ.

Of course, God does not call everyone to be missionaries or ministers of the church. He may call us to serve him as housewives, joiners, engineers, bank clerks, nurses, teachers or businessmen, and service for Christ in these callings is in no way inferior. But whatever our sphere of service, the loss of a sense of vocation is due, in no small measure, to the loss of assurance of salvation. Insecure Christians are bound to suffer from a lack of direction and purpose which will inevitably lead to aimlessness, lost opportunities, and yes — even spending their lives in the wrong job.

Little interest in the Bible

A funeral service had just ended and I was asked by the daughter of the deceased woman to read her will in the presence of the mourners. It was the mother's wish that this should be done and her daughter was naturally reluctant to do it herself. There were many beneficiaries, and the will began with the person who was to receive the largest sum and ended with the person who was to receive the smallest. When I stood to my feet and announced that I had been asked to read the will, the conversation ceased abruptly and the atmosphere became tense. I gained the impression that everyone present was hoping that his or her name would be mentioned, and preferably nearer the top of the list of names than the bottom. When I reached the end it was obvious that some were bitterly disappointed. I have never had a more attentive audience during my entire ministry! These people were clearly far more interested in the contents of the will than they had been in the sermon I had just preached.

The Bible reveals God's will to us and we are his beneficiaries. It tells us about the glorious riches which are ours in Christ (Colossians 1:27). It tells us that our inheritance is one that can never perish, spoil or fade (1 Peter 1:3,4). It tells us that 'Christ is the mediator of a new covenant, that those who are called may receive the promised inheritance — now that he has died as a ransom to set them free ...' (Hebrews 9:15). Of course, God is not dead, and the Bible doesn't mention our names, but it does tell us how we can be sure we are beneficiaries under the terms of the will. That's what assurance is all about. And that's why it is so important for Christians to study the Bible.

How then can we, who belong to God's family, claim to have a keen interest in our eternal inheritance if we do not also have a keen interest in the Bible? God has not left us in suspense like those mourners at the funeral; we do not have to sit biting our fingernails, waiting to find out whether we are in the will or not; it is always available for our inspection. If we are not eager to study it, what else can it mean but that we are not particularly interested?

The Bible also tells us how the citizens of heaven should live in this world. It tells us that our lives are bound up with God's will for time as well as eternity and that our future destiny cannot be separated from our present duty. If we are not eager to learn about both, we shall not be eager to learn about either.

In the morning, when I pick up my mail, I look first for the interesting items, especially letters from friends. I leave the large brown envelopes and the advertisments until last. I give most of these little more than a passing glance. Why do I do this? Because I am more interested in news from people I know and love than I am in communications from people who are unknown to me.

So it is with God's Word to us. When we enjoy a living relationship with him we cannot help loving his Word. We love it because we know and love the Author and we are always eager to know what he has to say to us and to learn what he wants us to do. His promises to us are sweeter than honey to our taste (Psalm 119:103). If this is not the case with us, we cannot know very much about the blessing of assurance.

Worldliness

'Christians who are too heavenly minded are of no earthly use!' So say the critics. It is simply not true. In fact, the opposite is the case. The more heavenly minded we are, the more earthly use we shall be. It is not heavenly mindedness that robs us of our usefulness, but earthly mindedness — conforming to the pattern of this world; to the attitudes of unbelievers. The more uncertain we are about our heavenly citizenship (Philippians 3:20), the more we are likely to conform to the life-styles of this world (Romans 12:2). It is possible, of course, for a believer to live with his 'head in the clouds', but this is absent mindedness, not heavenly mindedness.

In the sermon on the mount, Jesus teaches his disciples about the importance of having treasures in heaven. 'For where your treasure is', he says, 'there will your heart be also' (Matthew 6:20, 21). He also tells them they are 'the salt of the earth' and 'the light of the world' (Matthew 5:13,14). There is no suggestion here that having our hearts set on heavenly treasures will interfere with our earthly usefulness. On the contrary, Jesus is teaching us that if we are to be salt and light in this world, our hearts must be where our treasure is — in heaven!

The apostle Paul teaches the same lesson. He says to the Christians in Colosse, 'Since then, you have been raised with Christ, set your hearts on things above, where Christ is seated at the right hand of God. Set your minds on things above, not on earthly things' (Colossians 3:1, 2). In the rest of his letter he goes on to give wholesome teaching on practical Christian living. Like Jesus, Paul too sees heavenly mindedness as basic to earthly usefulness.

Fifty years ago, worldliness was defined in many Christian circles as drinking alchohol or going to the cinema or dance hall. When I was in my 'teens' I remember being told by some older would-be counsellors, that if I wanted to go on with the Lord I must avoid such places at all costs. I have vivid recollections of one zealous friend explaining the first verse of the first Psalm to me — 'Blessed is the man who does not walk in the counsel of the wicked or stand in the way of sinners or sit in the seat of mockers.' 'When you go to the cinema', he insisted, 'you do all three — you walk to the building with the wicked, you stand in the queue with the sinners and you sit down to watch the film with the mockers.' Thankfully, such unhelpful ideas have been set aside by further study of Bible teaching.

But what have we put in their place? The pendulum has now swung so far in the opposite direction, few Christians have any clear understanding of what worldliness is, or of its dangers, and many do not seem to care. They have adopted a lifestyle which is not far removed from that of many unbelievers.

35

Looking back on the teaching I was given so many years ago, I am amazed now that the clear definition of worldliness given by the apostle John was then so easily overlooked. 'Do not love the world', he says, 'or anything in the world. If anyone loves the world, the love of the Father is not in him. For everything in the world — the cravings of sinful man, the lust of his eyes and the boasting of what he has and does — comes not from the Father but from the world' (1 John 2:16). Clearly, worldliness is about covetous desires, being captivated by material things, and being proud of what we are and what we have. It is about our attitude to money, position and possessions.

Insecurity is one of the main reasons why so many Christians are worldly. They are but dimly aware that they are predestined to be like Jesus (Romans 8:29), and there is, therefore, little incentive to live pure and holy lives (1 John 3:3). Being vague about their high and holy calling, they cannot see what is in their own best interests. Their eyes are fixed on what is temporary rather than on what is unseen and eternal (2 Corinthians 4: 18).

According to the writer to the Hebrews, the Old Testament men and women of faith were 'longing for a better country — a heavenly one,' and for that reason they saw themselves as aliens and strangers on earth (Hebrews 11:13-16). Moses 'regarded disgrace for the sake of Christ as of greater value than the treasures of Egypt because he was looking ahead to his reward' (Hebrews 11:26). If we do not have this assurance of the 'better country' we shall find it hard to see this world in its true perspective. If we are not sure about our place in the world to come, what pressing reason do we have for feeling at odds with this present one?

Key points of chapter three — the causes of insecurity

- neglect of means of grace
- ignorance of the Bible
- misdirected prayer
- doubting
- yielding to temptation
- cherishing sin
- false teaching
- deficient teaching
- suffering

3.
The causes of insecurity

Neglect of the means of grace

The 'means of grace' are the channels through which God blesses his people — Bible-study, prayer, the ministry of the Word, worship, fellowship and the sacraments (baptism and communion)— without which it would be impossible to grow in grace. God may occasionally use other ways of promoting spiritual growth if he so chooses but to do so would be an exception.

There can be little doubt that a serious lack of discipline in the use of the means of grace is the main cause of insecurity. In many places Christians are not well taught; their attendance at worship and the Lord's table is haphazard and often a sterile routine. Prayer is not a priority, and the Lord's day is abused. They may be prosperous in the eyes of this world and physically fit, but their souls are not growing in spiritual strength (3 John 2). Unless these serious omissions are made good there is no point in looking elsewhere for the causes of spiritual insecurity. If other causes exist, the diligent use of the means of grace will bring them to light.

We all know what happens when we neglect our physical health. Under normal circumstances, if we eat sensibly, take adequate sleep and exercise, and do not abuse our bodies, we shall keep fit. But if we eat too much, exercise and sleep too little, we shall grow fat and get tired. Our spiritual health — which is much more important, because it holds 'promise for both the present life and the life to come' (1 Timothy 4: 8) — also depends on a regular use of the means God has provided. We need the constant nourishment of his Word, the encouragement of fellowship, the exercise of prayer and worship, the refreshment of rest from physical work. Daily discipline is vital because temporary lapses easily become permanent habits, and our strength can be drained without our being aware of it (Hosea 7:9).

When my wife calls me for dinner I am nearly always busy, and the temptation to continue what I am doing is strong. I know from experience that the food will be good, but the temptation is always easier to overcome when the appetising smell of the food actually reaches my nose. If I don't respond when called, whose fault is it that I go hungry? And whose fault is it if my spiritual hunger is not satisfied and my soul undernourished? We have tasted and seen that the LORD is good (Psalm 34:8). We know our heavenly Father has made rich provision and calls us to come and dine. If we don't respond, whom can we blame but ourselves? (John 6:35).

The importance of the means of grace is stressed in the New Testament. The apostle Paul says we are to 'let the Word of Christ dwell in us richly as we teach and admonish one another with all wisdom, and as we sing psalms, hymns and spiritual songs with gratitude in our hearts to God' (Colossians 3:16). The writer to the Hebrews says we are not to 'give up meeting together, as some are in the habit of doing,' but we are to 'encourage one another' (Hebrews 10:25). We are to 'pray continually' (1 Thessalonians 5:17). We are to take the Lord's Supper as a matter of loving obedience to the command of the Lord Jesus Christ himself (Luke 22: 17-20; 1 Corinthians 11:23-26).

The three thousand people who were added to the church on the day of Pentecost, 'devoted themselves to the apostles' teaching and to the fellowship, to the breaking of bread and to prayer' (Acts 2:42). It was by using these means that they grew in grace and in the knowledge of the truth. The significance of this must not be overlooked. The Holy Spirit did not ignore the usual means of grace (as many today expect him to do) but impressed their importance on the hearts of the new converts. Christians can, of course, be deprived of spiritual food through no fault of their own. They may be chronic invalids or elderly. Their local church may be lukewarm or dead. But deprivation and negligence are not the same thing. When we are deprived, but make good use of what remains available to us — as David did when he was in the desert of Judah (Psalm 63:1-4) — God has his own way of giving us healthy growth. But when we deliberately neglect a plentiful supply, we always lose out. 'The sluggard craves and gets nothing, but the desires of the diligent are fully satisfied' (Proverbs 13:4).

Ignorance of the Bible

Christians who are not well acquainted with the Bible cannot feel secure. The precious truths which provide the solid basis for our faith are all contained within the pages of Holy Scripture and the widespread ignorance and vagueness about these truths among believers is a principal cause of lack of assurance.

The delights of assurance are given to the child of God by the Spirit of God through the Word of God. But we are not passive in the process. Unless our minds are full of the Word of the Lord, our hearts will know little of the joy of the Lord. In other words, to know Christ better, we must know his Word better. 'Great peace have they who love God's law, and nothing can make them stumble' (Psalm 119:165).

Since my retirement I have been asked to preach in many different churches and I have been astonished to discover what little regard there is for the Bible in many of them. The people who attend have evidently been deprived of biblical preaching

and teaching for many years. In one church, I preached on the
two advents of Christ, explaining as simply as I could that
Christ came the first time to save, and is coming the second
time to judge. After the service an elderly man, who was a
regular worshipper, asked, 'Where did you get all that from?'
I explained that it was all in the Book, but he did not appear to
know which book I was referring to. In another church, as I
was shaking hands at the door, a lady (who turned out to be the
headmistress of the local school) commented, 'What a refreshing
change to hear a sermon from the Bible.' 'Sermons don't come
from anywhere else', I replied. 'They do here', she said. In yet
another case, a worshipper said to me after the service, 'You've
no idea what it means to me to hear the Word of God preached
from *that* pulpit.' Even in churches which claim to be
evangelical, I have not found many who are really hungry for
the Word of God, and some of those who are, have to listen to
the ministry of men who no longer give priority to preaching
and teaching (2 Timothy 4:1-5).

Decline in the private reading of the Bible has made matters
worse. Many Christians still use published notes as an aid to
daily reading, but that is frequently confined to a few hurried
minutes early morning or late evening and sometimes overlooked
altogether. Others have given up the habit and never open their
Bibles from one Sunday to the next.

Jesus gave his disciples the words of God so that they would
know with certainty that he came from God (John 17: 8). By
believing the truths revealed to them, they were persuaded that
he was the Messiah. All their remaining doubts were banished.
The truths which Jesus gave to them are also given to us, so
that our doubts may also be banished. Neglect of the Bible is
bound to lead to insecurity.

Misdirected prayer

The Bible tells us how to pray and what to pray for. So to pray well, we must know the Bible well. If the Bible does not guide us in what to pray for, we will be dominated by our own temporal interests and physical needs. Our prayers will tend to be haphazard and speculative and we shall be in danger of wasting our time trying to persuade our Heavenly Father to give us things he has not promised. Instead of growing in confidence, our doubts will be aggravated by unanswered prayers. If, on the other hand, we have an ever increasing knowledge of God's Word, we shall find ourselves praying more and more according to God's will. Since such prayers are always answered, our confidence will increase.

Some will not agree with this. They think that Christians have a right to expect God to give them whatever they want. They are eager to point out that Jesus promised his disciples that they would receive *whatever* they asked if only they believed (Matthew 21:22) and that *nothing* would be impossible to them (Matthew 17:20). But to take the words of Jesus in this way is a serious mistake and contradicts what is taught elsewhere in Scripture. It also ignores the essential conditions for prayer (1 John 5:14). Sooner or later, this approach will lead to more uncertainty. The words *whatever* and *nothing* do not provide us with a blank cheque on which to write our demands. On the contrary, they provide us with a precious safeguard — *whatever* comes within the range of God's love and wisdom, also comes within the range of prayer, and *nothing* is excluded.

After all, it is in the nature of faith to conform to God's will and to respond to his promises. Faith does not expect to receive anything from God unless it has reason to believe he will be pleased to grant it. Of course, there are many areas of our lives where we cannot be sure what God's will is. In these circumstances, faith rests content that God will not grant a petition unless it is his will to do so. We should rejoice that

God gives us such protection from the consequences of our ignorance (Proverbs 3:5, 6).

Surely, the primary purpose of prayer is that we may know God better. This is very clear in the prayers of the apostle Paul. He tells the believers in Ephesus, 'ever since I heard about your faith ... I have not stopped giving thanks for you, remembering you in my prayers. I keep asking that the God of our Lord Jesus Christ, the glorious Father, may give you the Spirit of wisdom and revelation, so that you may know him better. I pray also that the eyes of your hearts may be enlightened in order that you may know the hope to which he has called you ...' (Ephesians 1:15-18). 'I pray that out of his glorious riches he may strengthen you with power through his Spirit in your inner being, so that Christ may dwell in your hearts through faith. And I pray that you, being rooted and established in love, may have power, together with all the saints, to grasp how wide and long and high and deep is the love of Christ, and to know this love that surpasses knowledge - that you may be filled to the measure of all the fulness of God' (Ephesians 3:16-19). Our prayers lack discernment if this is not their central theme, because if we are to have the ability to 'distinguish good from evil' (Hebrews 5:14) and to 'discern what is best' (Philippians 1:10), growth in the knowledge of God is essential. If our temporal good (as we see it) is always the starting point, rather than our spiritual good (as God reveals it), our prayers are back to front.

We have no way of knowing what Christians pray for in private, but if our public prayers are anything to go by, most of us are at fault in this matter. We pray often for things like the healing of someone who is suffering from illness, or for a fine day for the church outing, or for money to repair the church roof — all of which are legitimate topics in their place — but we seldom pray for our hearts to be enlightened so that we may know the hope to which God has called us. Can there be any wonder that we feel insecure?

Doubting

When Tom asked Mary to marry him, he told her he could not live without her and that he would never have eyes for anyone else. For years Mary had been longing for a happy marriage relationship and she was thrilled with Tom's proposal. But then she started to have doubts. There were two causes. She was afraid Tom might break his promise, and she was not sure that she herself would make a good marriage partner. As a result, the happiness of a stable relationship eluded her.

Uncertainty in our relationship with God has similar causes. Either we do not believe God will be true to his Word, or we are not sure we have the ability to remain faithful to him. As long as either condition continues, the joy of a secure relationship will continue to elude us. Yet the truth is, we have no good reason for doubts, in either case. God has called us by his grace into a loving relationship with himself and has promised to keep us secure in his love forever.

Of course, as we saw earlier, even the most secure believer will have momentary doubts. But they are not serious. Like potholes in the road, they cause a little discomfort on the journey but do no permanent damage to the hope of arriving safely. But a constant nagging uncertainty about God's faithfulness to his promise, or about his power to keep us, is far more destructive. It limits our joy, confines our hope, and slows our spiritual progress.

Doubting God in this way is the result of using our judgment in a faithless manner. Instead of relying wholly on his faithfulness as we are called to do, we see difficulties which seem to be against his promise being fulfilled and think some things impossible for him. The two perplexed disciples who walked to Emmaus had this problem. They felt they had good reason to doubt, because the one who they thought was going to redeem Israel had been crucified. Things had gone hopelessly wrong—or so it seemed. What caused their perplexity? Jesus himself explained— 'how foolish you are', he said, 'and how slow of heart to believe all that the prophets have spoken!' (Luke 24:13-32).

The disciple Peter had the same problem. Jesus invited him to walk on the water, but when he saw the wind, he was afraid and began to sink. But it wasn't the wind that caused his problem. It was his doubts. 'You of little faith', Jesus said, 'why did you doubt?' (Matthew 14: 25-31).

Abraham will teach us how to overcome this difficulty. He believed God's promise to give him a son, and yet he entertained doubts because he and his wife were too old (Genesis 17:17). How did he triumph over his doubts? Did he keep on thinking about the impossibility? On the contrary, 'he considered him faithful who had made the promise' (Hebrews 11:11). From a doubter's point of view, God's promises are always made 'against the odds' as we say, but we who are Abraham's children, should follow our father's example (Romans 4:16).

Doubting is seen by some as an essential part of living faith and something to be proud of. But we must not be deceived. Unbelief is a sin which makes God angry. Remember the children of Israel; God brought them out of bondage and promised them a land flowing with milk and honey, but it soon became evident that they did not believe he was able to do what he had promised. Therefore, the message they heard was of no value to them, because they 'did not combine it with faith' (Hebrews 3:7 - 4: 3).

Yielding to temptation [1]

Temptation is 'common to man' (1 Corinthians 10:13) and should never of itself cause God's children to feel insecure. Indeed, knowing how to deal with temptation can be the means of strengthening our faith. Yielding to temptation, however, is a very different matter, and is a frequent cause of spiritual uncertainty among believers.

45

Today, we think of temptation as an evil thing, coming either from Satan or from our own lusts. We think of it as meaning 'enticed' or 'seduced'. But originally it meant 'to test' or 'to try' and God was seen as the one who tempted (tested) his children. In the older versions of the English Bible we read that 'God did tempt Abraham' (Genesis 22:1.AV), but in modern versions it has been changed to 'God tested Abraham.' This is because the word 'tempt' has changed its meaning and the idea of God tempting his children now creates problems for modern readers. Of course, it still depends where the temptation or the testing comes from. If it comes from our heavenly Father, his purpose is good and he intends to build up our faith, but if it comes from Satan, his purpose is evil and he intends to destroy our faith. Even so, without God's permission, Satan can do nothing, so that even Satan's evil designs are put to good use by God.

When Satan tempted Simon Peter, Jesus told him in advance what was going on behind the scenes: 'Simon, Simon, Satan has asked to sift you as wheat. But I have prayed for you, Simon, that your faith may not fail' (Luke 22:31,32). As wheat is shaken to get rid of the chaff, so Peter was going to be shaken to get rid of his corruptions. Satan was acting by divine permission and Peter was never in any real danger.

So if we feel insecure as a result of giving-in to temptation, who is to blame? We cannot blame God. The apostle James warns us not to do that: 'No-one should say, "God is tempting me." For God cannot be tempted with evil, nor does he tempt anyone' (James 1:13). James is not contradicting what is said elsewhere in the Bible. He is telling us that God never puts anyone to the test with the intention of causing him or her to sin, because that is contrary to God's nature. In any case, God has promised not only to keep us from being tempted beyond what we can bear but 'he will also provide a way out' so that we can stand up under it (1 Corinthians 10:13).

Since Satan's temptations are under God's control, we cannot blame Satan either (Job 1: 12; 2: 6). When she was naughty, one of my children used to try and blame Satan. She would look at me, and say confidently, 'It's not me daddy, it's the devil.' My reply was always the same — 'but it's your fault for listening to him.'

The apostle James tells us that 'each one is tempted when, by his own evil desire, he is dragged away and enticed. Then, after desire has conceived, it gives birth to sin ...' (James 1:14). James is not denying that Satan tempts us; he is simply warning us not to blame someone else when we yield. The fault is ours.

Yielding to temptation is often the result of walking deliberately into it. And walking into temptation is the result of thinking we can safely determine the limits of our strength. We may enjoy taking risks and tell ourselves that we will come to no harm. My friend Bill was a drunkard and his personal and family life were in ruins. I remember the shock I had when I first called at his home only a few days after his conversion. The wallpaper was hanging from the walls, the carpet was threadbare, and almost every key of the piano had been burnt by cigarette ends. I had a bigger surprise a few months later when I called again. The transformation was complete — new décor, new carpets, even a new piano. I was delighted that Bill had been able to conquer his drinking habit so easily. However, talking to his son later, I learned that Bill did not find it at all easy. He couldn't even trust himself to walk past the door of the place where he used to drink, and since his conversion had been in the habit of making a detour round the back streets to avoid that temptation.

Temptation can be strong and persistent and we may have to fight long and hard to overcome it. It may expose our weakness so much that we ask ourselves in astonishment, 'How can I, a redeemed child of God, be tempted to do this thing? How can I grieve my Lord by entertaining such evil thoughts?' In these circumstances it is easy to think ours is a special case and that we have more reason than others to excuse ourselves. But it is a serious mistake. As we have seen, there are no special cases. Temptation is 'common to all' (1 Corinthians 10:13).

When we play with temptation, we set events in motion that we may find difficult to stop. When we aggravate an already difficult situation by failing to run from it (when avoiding it is a clear option), our strength to fight is weakened, our resistance is lowered, and our conscience is defiled. The joy of salvation is immediately lost (Psalm 51:12). However, for the true child of God, the situation is never beyond the grace of God. Providing our repentance is genuine — which means being willing to turn from the sin and put right, as far as is humanly possible, what we have done wrong—our joy may be restored. 'Though I have fallen, I will rise ... because I have sinned against him, I will bear the Lord's wrath, until he pleads my case and establishes my right. He will bring me out into the light; I will see his justice' (Micah 7:8, 9).

We live at a time when sin is not taken seriously. The permissive society in which we live thinks little of sin and is seldom ashamed of it. Although the pressure on Christians to conform is constant and unrelenting (Romans 12:2), in every situation 'the Lord knows how to rescue the godly from trials' (2 Peter 2:9) and to 'make the righteous secure' (Psalm 7:9).

Cherishing sin

'All have sinned' (Romans 3:23) and Christians should be the first to admit the truth of that. For 'if we claim to be without sin, we deceive ourselves and the truth is not in us'   (1 John 1:8). But what a forgiving God we have! - 'If we confess our sins, he is faithful and just to forgive our sins and purify us from all unrighteousness' (1 John 1: 9). This means that all our sins, however odious, may be forgiven. It means that the wrong things we have done and the right things we have not done are removed from the record. It means that those sins we have fallen into again and again because of our weakness, will not be laid to our charge. It means that our open sins and our secret sins, our habitual sins and sins that result from sudden lapses, are all washed away. It means that the sins of anger, pride, jealousy, hypocrisy, selfish indulgence and impurity — yes, even adultery and murder (2 Samuel 12) — are all pardoned. No sin is beyond the reach of God's forgiveness except the sin of blasphemy against the Holy Spirit (Matthew 12:31) and true believers cannot be guilty of that.

Before we came to Christ, our sins did not trouble us very much and most of us thought we were as good as other people. But now we hate to sin. We readily echo the words of the apostle Paul, 'I know that nothing good lives in me, that is, in my sinful nature. For I have the desire to do what is good, but I cannot carry it out ... What a wretched man I am! Who will rescue me from this body of death?' (Romans 7: 18,24). This conflict with sin will go on as long as we live, because our 'sinful nature desires what is contrary to the Spirit, and the Spirit what is contrary to the sinful nature. They are in conflict with each other ...' (Galatians 5:17).

Consciousness of sin and confidence in God always go together. An assured heart is always a contrite heart. If we acknowledge our transgressions daily and cry to God for strength to overcome them, no sin should ever make us feel insecure. The memories of our past sins will cause us grief but they should never rob us of our assurance, no matter how grievous they were.

A cherished sin is different. It is a sin that I love and obstinately refuse to give up. It is a sin which scorns God's gracious forgiveness. By cherishing it, I am, in effect, giving that particular sin the power to weaken, or even destroy my assurance. I am allowing it to come between me and God, so that I cannot pray with confidence. If I try to pray, I find I am talking to myself, for if I cherish sin in my heart, the Lord does not listen (Psalm 66:18). No, I have not lost my salvation, if

49

my conversion was a true one, but I have certainly lost the enjoyment and assurance I could know. God will never let me go, but neither will he let me go on sinning in peace. He loves me too much for that.

It is amazing what lengths we Christians will go to when we are determined to justify a particular sin. We try to persuade ourselves that it isn't important. We argue that it doesn't matter because we are doing so well in other ways. We insist that we can't manage to live without the pleasure it affords. And in any case, nobody is perfect, we say, in order to excuse ourselves! But all those arguments achieve nothing. A disease in one part of my body affects the whole, and one cherished sin in my life weakens my general spiritual health. There are no exceptions to the Lord's command, 'Be holy, because I am holy' (1 Peter 1:16) and there must be no excuses. 'Whoever keeps the whole law and yet stumbles at just one point is guilty of breaking all of it' (James 2:10).

False teaching

Ever since the church was founded, the security of believers has been threatened by false teachers. Paul warned young Timothy about two men called Hymenaeus and Philetus who denied the resurrection of the body and were destroying the faith of some (2 Timothy 2:17, 18). He warned Titus about those who, 'for the sake of dishonest gain' were 'ruining whole households' by teaching things they ought not to teach (Titus 1:11). He warned the Colossians against being deceived by 'fine-sounding arguments' and so being taken captive 'through hollow and deceptive philosophy' (Colossians 2:4, 8). The apostle John warned against the 'many deceivers, who do not acknowledge Jesus Christ as coming in the flesh ... Watch out', he says, 'that you do not lose what you have worked for' (2 John 7, 8).

All these false teachers have their modern counterparts, whose teaching, though different in many ways, has the same effect — the confidence of Christians, especially those who are not well grounded in the faith, is shaken. They are confused by church leaders who deny the Christian creeds; they are under pressure to doubt the genuineness of their conversion from preachers who insist on the necessity of certain post-conversion experiences; they are bewildered by ministers who put reason before revelation, and theory before truth (Colossians 2:8). The apostle Peter's warning is still relevant — 'Be on your guard so that you may not be carried away by the error of lawless men and fall from your secure position' (2 Peter 3:17).

What a comfort it is to know that those whom God has chosen can never be completely deceived by false teaching! Jesus tells us that 'many false prophets will appear and deceive many people' and they will even 'perform great signs and miracles to deceive even the elect ... *if that were possible'* (Matthew 24:11, 24). But for the fact that God chose us in Christ 'before the creation of the world to be holy and blameless in his sight' (Ephesians 1:4), believers would be as vulnerable as anyone else.

Deficient teaching

The secure position of believers is threatened just as much, if not more, by deficient and unbalanced teaching, as it is by false teaching. Teachers who are obsessed with one aspect of the truth at the expense of others are bound to leave their pupils with gaps in their knowledge. Indeed, much of the blame for the widespread lack of confidence among believers must be laid at the door of pastors and teachers who obscure the truth by attaching too much importance to secondary matters — like the young lady who was presented by her suitor with a very expensive engagement ring and being more taken with the ring-case than the ring, exclaimed, 'O what a lovely box'!

Preachers who are more enthusiastic about their favourite subjects and personal theories than they are about contending 'for the faith that was once entrusted to the saints' (Jude 3), have lost their way. Christians who listen to the ministry of these people are unlikely to grow in assurance because they are not being grounded in the great truths on which their assurance rests.

If, for instance, believers are not well taught about the meaning of grace (Ephesians 2:8), they will be in constant danger of believing they must contribute something towards their own salvation. If they are not instructed about the divine origin of their salvation (Ephesians 1:4), they will go on thinking they initiated it themselves. If they are not told that in Christ they have everything (Colossians 2:10), they will go on searching for something else, although they possess everything needful.

Teaching can be deficient in quantity as well as quality. The feeble faith of many is due to a lack of nourishment. They receive the right kind of food but have to subsist on a very meagre diet. Their teachers are either lazy, or have allowed themselves to be intimidated by people who have no hunger for the Word of God and who think a good sermon is one that lasts no more than ten minutes. They have allowed people with little or no appetite for the Word of God to determine the spiritual food given to everyone else. Week after week the hungry are sent away empty.

Suffering

Without doubt, severe trials do sometimes cause Christians to lose their assurance. But is the trial their own fault or did God intend it? Some argue that our loving Father would never take our assurance away intentionally, but others think there are some lessons he cannot teach us in any other way. The fact that suffering may cause us to feel deserted by God does not, of course, prove that this was his intention. Perhaps we were not firmly established in the first place and now our weakness is being exposed in the hour of crisis. Insecurity may lie hidden for many years behind good physical health and material prosperity.

The problem is aggravated by the fact that some forms of suffering impair our faculties and make it difficult for us to know how we feel about our relationship with God. After being a Christian for about forty years, without experiencing any serious loss of confidence, I was taken seriously ill. I was seized by severe pain and panic, and I began to feel that everything I had learned about trusting God had suddenly become academic. My doctor couldn't find anything to relieve the pain, and to my astonishment, I couldn't control the panic. As the attacks came and went, my spirit went up and down like a yo-yo. I couldn't eat or sleep properly; I couldn't concentrate; I couldn't take pleasure in anything. If you had asked me if I felt God had deserted me, I would not have been able to give a firm answer one way or the other. I was too ill to think clearly. Even now my memory of the experience is cloudy. One thing, however, is quite certain — when I began to recover, the realisation that I was God's child filled me with greater joy than ever.

The Bible certainly teaches that God allows his children to be tested by trials and tribulations and that they are sometimes severe. It may be an illness or a bitter personal tragedy as in the case of Job, or it may be a handicap of some sort as in the case of Paul (2 Corinthians 12:7-9). But does the Bible teach that God *deliberately* removes the assurance of our salvation? The interesting thing about Job is that, although he did not know it at the time, his confidence in God was being tested in order to demonstrate God's confidence in him (Job 1:9-12). However, although Job spoke 'words without knowledge' (Job 38:2) during his distress, there is nothing to suggest that he ever lost his assurance. On the contrary, even in the depths of his agony he was able to say 'I know that my Redeemer lives

... and after my skin has been destroyed ... I will see God' (Job 19:26). Paul's plea for the 'thorn in the flesh' to be removed was refused, but his assurance was not weakened. The Lord said to him, 'My grace is sufficient for you, for my power is made perfect in weakness' (2 Corinthians 12:9).

The writers of the Psalms have a lot to say about personal anguish during severe trials. 'When I was in distress, I sought the Lord; at night I stretched out untiring hands and my soul refused to be comforted' (Psalm 77:2). 'In my alarm I said, "I am cut off from your sight!" ' (Psalm 31:22). 'How long, O Lord: Will you hide yourself for ever?' (Psalm 89:46). These words certainly describe a sense of desolation, but do they suggest a feeling of desertion as well? I think not. Looking back on his suffering, the writer of Psalm 119 was able to say, 'It was good for me to be afflicted so that I might learn your decrees' (Psalm 119:71). David speaks of being rejected and loved at the same time! (Psalm 60:1,5).

I recall vividly the feeling of fear and desolation I felt when, as a child, I became separated from my parents in a strange town. I did not doubt their love for a moment and I knew they would be deeply concerned about me. Similarly the child of God may feel desolate, but should never feel abandoned.

The apostle Peter tells us that our trials may cause us grief but they come so that our faith 'of greater worth than gold ... may be proved to be genuine and may result in praise, glory and honour when Jesus Christ is revealed' (1 Peter 1:7). 'We know' says Paul, 'that suffering produces perseverance; perseverance, character; and character, hope' (Romans 5:3). In the light of all the Bible's teaching on the subject we may be confident that although suffering may cause loss of assurance, it is not God's intention that it should.

Note 1. *Temptation.* Readers may like to know of the book '*What every Christian needs to know*', ISBN 0-946462-47X, also published by Grace Publications, dealing at length with this subject, based on a work by the great Puritan writer, John Owen.

Key points of chapter four — false security

- formal religion
- folklore
- self-righteousness
- presumption

4.
False security

Formal religion

People may claim to be Christian and feel confident about going to heaven, and yet be deceived. Instead of relying on what Christ has done, they put their trust in themselves and in what they have done. Such a person is in a very dangerous position. 'What he trusts in is fragile, what he relies on is a spider's web. He leans on his web; he clings to it, but it does not hold' (Job 8:13-15).

Many base their hopes on their habitual performance of religious duties. They go through the forms of ceremonies of the church, but without life, joy or enlightenment. The security they feel does not come through God's Word, the fellowship, or sharing in the communion service, but from familiarity with the forms of worship, the church architecture, the singing of the choir and so on.

A Roman Catholic woman once came to ask me if she could join the church of which I was minister.

'Why have you decided to leave your own Church?' I asked.

'The priest has started saying the mass [1] in English' she explained, 'and I think it's a load of rubbish.'

I jumped, far too hastily, to the conclusion that here was an intelligent woman who had become aware of the errors of the mass.

'What, in particular, do you not like about it?' I asked eagerly.
'I don't like any of it,' she replied.

Then, almost as an afterthought, she added:

'I have told the priest I shall not be coming back until he puts it back into Latin.'

For some, a merely formal approach to worship was instilled into them during their childhood — in the home, the school, or the church. Others were once concerned about their souls and challenged by the Word of God, but now the urgency has gone; only the sterile routine remains.

God hates formal, insincere religion. It is clearly condemned in Scripture. 'The Lord says: "These people come near to me with their mouth and honour me with their lips, but their hearts are far from me. Their worship is made up only of rules taught by men" ' (Isaiah 29:13). In the days of Amos the prophet, the religious ceremonies were being observed as strictly as ever. The people brought their offerings willingly and felt safe because they were standing on holy ground and going through well established routines. But God rejected their worship because they were not sincere with him. The people were merely going through the rituals, assuming that it would make them acceptable to God. 'Woe to you who are complacent in Zion,' says the prophet, 'and to you who feel secure on Mount Samaria' (Amos 5:21-24; 6:1).

Formal religion was condemned by Jesus too. Many of the Jews felt confident because they were the circumcised descendants of Abraham, the friend of God (James 2:23), and lived 'according to the tradition of the elders' but Jesus told them they were the slaves of sin (Mark 7:5-8; John 8:31-41).

John the Baptist also condemned the practice of religious routines which had no effect in the lives of worshippers. 'When he saw many of the Pharisees and Sadducees coming to where he was baptising, he said to them: "You brood of vipers! who warned you to flee from the coming wrath? Produce fruit in keeping with repentance. And do not think you can say to yourselves, 'We have Abraham as our father'" ' (Matthew 3:7-9).

These attitudes are still common among churchgoers today. A formal attachment to the church and an occasional attendance at Holy Communion provides many with a feeling of respectability and security, but there is no genuine repentance, no hunger for the Word of God, and no real change of heart. It is a form of godliness without power (2 Timothy 3:5).

Folklore

Religious folklore, or folk-religion as it is sometimes called, turns religion into superstition and legend. It uses pseudo-religious rites and gestures and tends to regard the services and sacraments of the church as a means of protection against misfortune. The vague sense of security it may offer to some is like a mist which quickly disappears.

In one district where I served as a minister it was not uncommon for women to come straight from the maternity hospital to the vicarage asking to be 'churched' [2] because they believed it would bring them misfortune to go home without having gone through that ritual. I remember a grandmother refusing to allow her daughter and new baby into the house because she had not been 'churched.' When the minister eventually arrived to sort out the problem, the young mother was sitting on a chair outside the front door in the driving snow, trying to keep her baby warm!

Truths about God are handed down from one generation to another and, in the absence of corrective teaching, those truths tend to get trivialised and sentimentalised in the process. The notion that God is good survives well in our society but only in the sense that he will look after me when I am in trouble, and will not interfere with me when things are going well. He will overlook my sins, and when I die he will take me to be with Jesus. Many cling to such ideas and will not allow them to be questioned, simply because they feel comfortable with them. On the other hand, the notion that God will bring sinners to judgement does not survive well because it is not thought to be a nice idea.

Behind all the false ideas of folk-religion there may be a vague realisation that it is not safe to ignore God altogether, but in spite of that no serious effort is made to discover what the truth is. God then becomes little more than a mental image, far removed from the God revealed in Scripture. The forming of such images in the mind is just as bad as cutting them out of wood or stone, and just as foolish. Both break the second commandment (Exodus 20:4).

Self-righteousness

Self-righteousness thrives wherever there is ignorance of the holiness of God and therefore of the seriousness of sin. Millions feel secure because they believe they are good enough for God to accept, just as they are. They achieve this by inflating their own imagined righteousness and belittling God's righteousness, in order to minimise the gap between, and by clinging to the notion that God is tolerant. If they should fall short at any point, he is always at hand to forgive, they think. The security this attitude affords is a most serious deception.

Making comparisons with people who are considered morally inferior is a favourite ploy of self-righteous individuals. They look down with self-satisfaction on people who are unprincipled, indecent or irreligious. In the judgement of such people few others occupy higher moral ground than they, and none can be better placed in the eyes of God than they! They are like terminally ill patients who take comfort in the thought that there are others in a worse state than themselves, but do not think about those who are very much better. Jesus told a parable 'to some who were confident of their own righteousness and looked down on everybody else.' In the story, a proud religious man tried to put himself in a good light by comparing himself with a despised tax-collector (well-known in the days of Jesus for extortion and malpractice). 'God, I thank you that I am not like other men - robbers, evil doers, adulterers - or even like this tax-collector.' But the tax-collector 'would not even look up to heaven, but beat upon his breast and said, "God have mercy on me, a sinner." This man' (i.e. the tax collector), said Jesus, 'rather than the other, went home justified before God' (Luke 18:9-14).

Another common device of the self-righteous is to appeal to those commandments they think they have kept and ignore the rest. Among the favourites many think they have kept are the two commandments forbidding adultery and murder. People may derive comfort from the thought that they have never actually committed either of these sins, and if they are aware of the teaching of Jesus about breaking these two commandments in our hearts, they prefer not to think about it (Matthew 5:22, 28).

Any attempt to establish our own righteousness only advertises the fact that we are strangers to the grace of God. True believers know that even their 'righteous acts are like filthy rags' in the sight of God (Isaiah 64:6) and are deeply grateful for the privilege of having received a 'righteousness from Go ... through faith in Jesus Christ' (Romans 3:22). 'For it is by grace you have been saved, through faith ... not by works, so that no-one can boast' (Ephesians 2:8).

Of course, we all have a duty always to do our best, but to build our hope on the idea that we can earn a place in heaven by our own righteousness is like trying to build castles in the air. 'So you also,' said Jesus, 'when you have done everything you were told to do, should say, "We are unworthy servants; we have only done our duty"' (Luke 17:10). Perfect obedience by us to God's commands is impossible and even our noblest actions will not stand the scrutiny of God's judgement. 'No-one will be declared righteous in his sight by observing the law.' 'There is no-one righteous, not even one' (Romans 3:10, 20). Nobody has ever been, or ever will be accepted by God on the basis of personal merit, for 'if righteousness could be gained through the law, Christ died for nothing!' (Galatians 2:21). 'God saved us, not because of righteous things we had done, but because of his mercy' (Titus 3:5).

Satisfaction with our own supposed righteousness closes our minds to God's precious gift of salvation. It gives false assurance to millions and keeps them in ignorance of their need of Christ. As Paul said of the Jews of his day: 'Since they did not know the righteousness that comes from God and sought to establish a righteousness of their own, they did not submit to God's righteousness' (Romans 10: 3).

Presumption

Behind all these false hopes lies the sin of presumption. The person who has a form of religion *presumes* his performance of religious duties will put him in God's favour. The superstitious person presumes his or her observance of certain religious rites and gestures will be to their advantage, and the self-righteous presume they are good enough to go to heaven in their own right.

A presumptuous person is someone who takes things for granted. In matters of religion, he is a person who thinks his own unverified ideas about God can be trusted. He bases his 'faith' on vague notions about the goodness of God. He makes peace *with himself* by ignoring the evidence of Scripture and stifling his conscience. Presumption knows no bounds. It can dispose of hell simply by regarding it as not a nice idea and it can turn heaven into a place where the wicked are at peace. The hope it offers is about as substantial as a pot of gold at the end of the rainbow i.e. no hope at all.

When facing important decisions in life, most people are wise enough not to presume anything. When they are sick they consult the doctor; when they are buying a house they call in a surveyor, and when buying a second-hand car they have it examined by a qualified engineer. Yet when it comes to the most vital matter of all — that of their eternal destiny — many are prepared to act on their presumptions and make no attempt whatsoever to discover the truth. The explanation for this foolish behaviour is not hard to find. A man does not have to swallow his pride when he consults the doctor, the surveyor, or the motor engineer. But Christianity deals with questions of sin and guilt and since the presumptuous person considers himself as well-informed as anyone else, he will not admit his need for guidance about salvation. His own judgement, he thinks, is as good as anyone else's and that is the end of the matter.

The sin of presumption prevented the children of Israel from entering the promised land. When the time came to capture the land, they refused to trust in God and trusted their own judgement instead. But when they heard about their punishment (not one of them would ever see the land), they changed their minds and decided to attack, 'Why are you disobeying the Lord's command?' Moses demanded. 'This will not succeed! Do not go up because the Lord is not with you. You will be defeated by your enemies.' But they persisted, and their presumption led to a humiliating defeat (Numbers 14). These things are written for our learning — our 'promised land' is to be gained, not by following our own presumptuous schemes, but by trusting in God's Word (Hebrews 4:1-3).

Presumption is sheer folly. We simply cannot afford to ignore what God has revealed, in favour of our own ideas. Our understanding is darkened because of the ignorance that is in us (Ephesians 4:18) and if we presume to go our own way, Christ will be of no value to us (Galatians 5:2). 'There is a way that seems right to a man but in the end it leads to death' (Proverbs 14:12).

So don't be deceived. 'Examine yourselves,' says the apostle Paul, 'to see whether you are in the faith; test yourselves. Do you not realise that Christ is in you — unless of course, you fail the test?' (2 Corinthians 13:5). The well-known Bible commentator Matthew Henry wisely applies Paul's demand to all who call themselves Christians. He says 'we should examine whether we be in the faith, because it is a matter in which we may be easily deceived.' Indeed it is! 'The heart is deceitful above all things' (Jeremiah 17:9).

Superficially, there are many similarities between true believers and nominal Christians. Both support the church; both attend its services, both receive baptism and the Lord's Supper, both accept the creeds. But the differences are considerable. Nominal Christians will not admit that their salvation depends entirely on Christ (Galatians 3:10-13), and because of this, the Lord Jesus Christ is not precious to them (1 Peter 2:7). Whatever profession they may make, they are not born of God (John 1:12,13) and therefore, their faith is merely intellectual and does not purify the heart (Acts 15:9). They know nothing about the inner testimony of the Spirit (1 John 5:9,10), take little delight in God's Word, and no pleasure in the fellowship of believers. They have no longing after holiness (Matthew 5:6), no desire to win others for Christ (2 Corinthians 5:20) and no willingness to suffer with him (Romans 8:17).

The apostle John gives us three basic tests of genuine assurance. The first is the test of obedience — 'We know we have come to know him if we obey his commands' (1 John 2:3). This doesn't mean we must be perfect before we can be sure; it means that evidence of the genuineness of our assurance is seen in our eagerness to base our lives on the teaching of God's Word.

The second is the test of love — 'We know that we have passed from death to life, because we love our brothers' (1 John 3:14). Love for our Christian brothers and sisters is proof of new life.

The third is the test of belief. John tells us that those who deny the truth do not really belong to the true church because 'no lie comes from the truth' (1 John 2:19-21). 'We also know that the Son of God has come and has given us understanding, so that we may know him who is true' (1 John 5:20).

In the day of judgement all pretence will be exposed. All who cling to false hopes will be excluded from the presence of God for ever. For when the Lord Jesus is revealed from heaven 'he will punish those who do not obey the gospel of our Lord Jesus. They will be punished with everlasting destruction and shut out from the presence of the Lord and from the majesty of his power on the day he comes to be glorified in his holy people and to be marvelled at among those who have believed' (2 Thessalonians 1:8-10).

All who hate knowledge and do not choose to fear the Lord 'will eat the fruit of their ways and be filled with the fruit of their schemes' (Proverbs 1:29-31). The false hopes of those who say: 'I will be safe, even though I persist in going my own way' (Deuteronomy 29:19) will come to nothing.

False hopes are like dreams; the fantasy does not give way to reality until the dreamer awakes. But then it may be too late. How important it is to wake up before the day of the Lord dawns! The day of judgement, says Isaiah, 'will come like destruction from the Almighty' and 'because of this, all hands will go limp, every man's heart will melt. Terror will seize them, pain and anguish will grip them' (Isaiah 13:6-8).

Let all who claim to be true Christians remember the solemn words of Jesus: 'Not everyone who says to me, "Lord, Lord" will enter the kingdom of heaven, but only he who does the will of my Father who is in heaven. Many will say to me on that day, "Lord, Lord, did we not prophesy in your name, and in your name drive out demons and perform many miracles?" Then I will tell them plainly, "I never knew you. Away from me, you evildoers!" ' (Matthew 7:21-23).

Note 1. *Mass.* The term commonly used in Roman Catholic and Anglo-Catholic churches for the Eucharist or Lord's Supper during which, it is said, the priest participates in the sacrifice of the body and blood of Christ, by the transubstantiation of the bread and wine. This view has never been accepted by Protestant churches.

Note 2. *Churched.* Going to a church to say the service of thanksgiving for childbirth, from the Book of Common Prayer of the Anglican church.

Key points of chapter five — the experience of assurance

- the Spirit's teaching
- the Spirit's testimony
- the Spirit's transformation

5.
The experience of assurance

The Spirit's teaching

When the Psalmist prayed, 'open my eyes that I may see wonderful things in your law' (Psalm 119:18), he was expressing a desire to discover truths in God's Word which he had not yet seen. But his eyes were not closed altogether. He already knew that God's Word contained wonderful things. Glimpses of truth had already thrilled his heart so much that he wanted to see more and more.

Before we became Christians, we were spiritually blinded by the god of this age, so that we could not understand the gospel (2 Corinthians 4:4). But now, the Holy Spirit has opened our spiritual 'eyes' to the truth of God's Word — the Bible — and through it, we have come alive to God, whose Word it is. As the apostle Peter puts it, we 'have been born again, not of perishable seed, but of imperishable, through the living and enduring word of God' (1 Peter 1:23). But we must not stop here; this is only the beginning. Like the Psalmist, we must go on asking God to open our eyes, so that we may see yet more wonderful things in his Word. Only by this means shall we grow into the 'full riches of complete understanding'

(Colossians 2:2). It is a process which depends on the Spirit's continuing to open the truth of the Scriptures to our minds.

Paul's first concern for the Christians in Ephesus was that they might be taught by the Spirit: 'I keep asking that the God of our Lord Jesus Christ, the glorious Father, may give you the Spirit of wisdom and revelation, so that you may know him better. I pray also that the eyes of your heart may be enlightened in order that you may know the hope to which he has called you, the riches of his glorious inheritance in the saints' (Ephesians 1: 17,18).

In this prayer, Paul is not asking God to reveal extra truths that his readers are to add to the truths of the gospel. He is praying that they will have a better understanding of the gospel they have already received. As far as we are concerned, the Scriptures contain all the truths we need in order to grow strong in the faith; we need to pray that the Spirit will continue to open our minds and hearts to their meaning and significance. Like a telescope that reveals stars that are already there, but which were not seen before, the Spirit continues to bring biblical truths which we had not previously appreciated into our understanding.

This activity of the Spirit confirms to our hearts that God's Word is true, so that we may be sure it is indeed the Word of God. By limiting himself to the use of what God's Word tells us, the Spirit is not unhappily restricted, as some seem to think. For if the Spirit added to the Word, it would mean that Scripture, which claims to make us 'wise for salvation through faith in Christ Jesus' (2 Timothy 3:15) is inadequate. And if the Spirit contradicted the Word it would mean that God is inconsistent with himself. Both notions are totally unacceptable. In any case, if we claim to have special revelations of truth which are not backed up by the Word of God, we have no way of proving them to be true.

Being taught by the Spirit is not merely learning more of the Bible by heart. There's a big difference between learning

Bible texts (which is not a bad thing to do) and being taught by the Spirit. I may know many of God's promises by heart, but if the Spirit does not open my understanding and influence my spirit, I am not enlightened. My mind may be informed, but my life is not transformed.

When I was a young soldier, an incident took place which made me realise the truth of this. I was fast asleep in an army hut with about twenty other soldiers. About midnight we were rudely awakened by a man who was standing, with some difficulty, on the top of a double bunk, shouting texts from the Bible — all from memory. He was drunk and his speech was slurred, but he was quoting text after text accurately. I knew him to be a profane man and I lay on my bunk wondering why such knowledge of Scripture had left him unmoved when, by comparison, my own life had been so profoundly changed. I was just beginning to realise how much I was indebted to the Holy Spirit for opening my understanding to the truth and so influencing my life.

Jesus promised that the Spirit of truth would guide us into all truth. The promise was made first to the apostles and it is a guarantee that what they taught is reliable and complete. It is important to notice that they were guided into all the truth concerning Jesus, as he goes on to explain: the Spirit 'will not speak on his own; he will speak only what he hears ... taking from what is mine and making it known to you' (John 16:13,14). This means that the apostles were guided to expand (but not to alter or add to) what Christ taught, especially about the way of salvation and the purpose of redemption. It is only Jesus who is the embodiment of truth (John 14:6).

The promise extends to us as well because the gift of the Spirit was not just for the apostles, but for the church. He will guide us into all the truth that is in Jesus (Ephesians 4: 21-24). That is, he will give us insight into all that he and the apostles taught about himself. 'It is written in the prophets' Jesus said, 'they shall all be taught by God' (John 6: 45).

Being taught by God is an exciting process. Day by day, as the Holy Spirit applies the Word of God to our minds and hearts, its power and its freshness give us great joy. We enter into an experience similar to that of the two disciples whose hearts were burning within them while Jesus opened the Scriptures to them (Luke 24:32). And our delight in the Word is always increasing. The entrance of God's Word gives us more and more light (Psalm 119:130), and the more light we have, so the more we rejoice. 'Oh, how I love your law! I meditate on it all day long' (Psalm 119:97).

If the disciples of Jesus, who used to read the Scriptures every Sabbath day, needed to have their minds opened 'so they could understand' (Luke 24:45), then so do we. Our assurance depends upon it.

The Spirit's testimony

'I tell you the truth,' Jesus said, 'whoever hears my word and believes him who sent me has eternal life and will not be condemned; he has crossed over from death to life' (John 5:24). When the Spirit gives us faith to believe such precious promises as this, what more do we need? Surely this should be enough. How can we go on feeling insecure in the light of such pledges?

Yet God in his mercy, knowing our weakness, gives us more. He gives us direct confirmation in our hearts that we are the children of God and, as such, inheritors of the promises. Again, there is always perfect agreement between what the Word promises and what the Spirit confirms. He neither adds to the Word, nor takes away from it.

'You did not receive a spirit that makes you a slave again to fear,' says Paul, 'but you received the Spirit of adoption (sonship). And by him we cry, "Abba, Father." ' ('Abba' means 'Father'). The Spirit himself testifies with our spirit that we are God's children' (Romans 8:15,16).

Words cannot describe how the Spirit gives us this spirit of

71

sonship. It is 'better felt than telt (told)', as they used to say in the area where I was born and brought up. A small boy would hardly be able to explain why he is able to relate so confidently to his dad. It is enough for him that he feels secure; questions like, 'How do you know that's your father?' never enter his head. How much greater is our inability to explain the spirit of sonship which God has given us? It is enough for us that we know it in our hearts.

Even so, we must try to understand it, even if only in part. John Owen, a Puritan preacher and teacher, compared the way the Holy Spirit assures us to a court case in which a man is trying to establish his claim to be a true son against strong opposition. Evidence and counter-evidence is presented, but things seem not to be going well for the claimant. Then, a reliable witness enters the court and gives powerful testimony on the claimant's behalf - and he wins his case. The reliable witness for believers is, of course, the Holy Spirit, and the courtroom is the heart of the believer. The claim to be a child of God is being opposed by the counter-claim of Satan but the Spirit's testimony puts the opposition to silence and the believer's claim is firmly established.

To explain it another way — I say to myself, 'I really do feel God has adopted me into his family. The evidence that I am a child of God is quite strong and agrees with Scripture teaching, but I am not yet fully persuaded.' At this point the Holy Spirit comes to me and gives a sense of assurance: 'Yes, you are a child of God.' To my great joy, I discover the Spirit is saying the same as my human spirit. Paul puts it like this: 'Because you are sons, God sent the Spirit of his Son into our hearts, the Spirit who calls out "Abba, Father"' (Galatians 4:6).

When the Spirit confirms our sonship in this way we are not left in any doubt about who is speaking and why. Those who have this inner assurance cannot question it. It takes them out of the realm of uncertainty and enables them to rejoice in their adoption as God's children. Those who do not have it cannot possibly know what we are talking about.

With the Spirit's assurance that we are God's children comes the assurance of our eternal inheritance. 'If we are children' says Paul, 'then we are heirs — heirs of God and co-heirs with Christ' (Romans 8:17). Our heavenly Father will make sure we do not fail to enter into our inheritance (1 Peter 1:5).

The Spirit's transformation

There is yet another confirmation of our status as the children of God. The testimony of the Spirit in our hearts is confirmed by the changes he makes in our lives. We are different; we know we are different, and we know we could not possibly have changed ourselves. Some of us tried to do so for years, without success. But now, the evidence of the new birth in our lives is plain.

But are we not guilty of self-righteousness when we look to ourselves for the evidence that we are God's children? No, not at all. We are not looking for natural goodness of which to boast but for spiritual graces for which to be thankful; graces we know have been given to us by the Spirit. In any case, now that we have trusted Christ we have renounced the notion that there is any merit in our own goodness.

This method of establishing our status is consistent with Scripture. As we have already seen, Paul urges us to examine ourselves to see whether, or not, we are 'in the faith' (2 Corinthians 13:5). When we do examine ourselves, we are firmly persuaded that we owe our new spiritual character to the grace of God. It was so with the apostle himself: 'By the grace of God I am what I am, and his grace to me was not without effect' (1 Corinthians 15:10). Paul was proud to say: 'Our conscience testifies that we have conducted ourselves in the world, and in our relations with you, in the holiness and sincerity that are from God' (2 Corinthians 1:12).

What then is the evidence of being God's child? We know we are the children of God because we obey his commands

(1 John 2:3), because we hate sin (1 John 3:9, 10), and because we love our fellow believers (1 John 3:14). Also, we want to know more about Jesus (Philippians 3:10) and we take delight in worship and fellowship (1 John 1:7). As his children, we talk to our heavenly Father with confidence (Philippians 4:6) and we grieve over our sins (Romans 7:24). We hunger and thirst after righteousness and purity; we want to be at peace with other people but we are willing to suffer, if need be, for the sake of Christ (Matthew 5:11-12; 1 Corinthians 4:11). When these characteristics, so foreign to our human nature, are in evidence, we know we are the spiritual children of God. No other conclusion is possible.

This evidence shows to be false those who say that since the promises of salvation are not made to anyone by name, it is impossible to be sure they apply to anyone individually. Abraham had cause to be sure, they say, because God called him by name, but God has not called us by name. But it really is not necessary for God to use our names because Scripture makes it quite clear who are the people to whom God's promises apply. Scripture identifies them, not by name, but by character; and with the judgment given by the Spirit they are able to draw the conclusion that they are the children of God to whom the promises apply. We know 'we are God's workmanship, created in Christ Jesus for good works, which God has prepared in advance for us to do' (Ephesians 2: 10).

In summary, we know we are God's children if God's Spirit has brought us to new birth through God's Word and by the same means he continues to enlighten us about the hope to which we are called. He gives us a conviction in our hearts that we are the children of God and confirms it by the evidence of our changed lives. All these evidences add up to an overwhelming assurance.

Key points of chapter six — the basis of assurance

- God's Word
- God's covenant
- God's oath
- God's verdict
- God's nature
- God's choice
- God's gift
- God's seal

6.
The basis of assurance

God's Word

I visited a woman who was dying from cancer. Her relatives had told her she would soon recover and, to try and convince her of this, they had promised to take her with them on holiday as soon as she was better. I was asked not to say anything to arouse her suspicions, but when I was alone with her she raised the matter of the holiday and asked me directly if she was going to get better. 'I know you will not deceive me' she said. The poor woman could take no pleasure in the prospect of a holiday, because she was not sure she could rely on the word of her well-meaning relatives. She had good reason to doubt what they said.

How different is our case, and how different are the promises of God. He cannot deceive us. 'Do not let your hearts be troubled,' Jesus said, 'Trust in God; trust also in me. In my Father's house are many rooms; if it were not so, I would have told you. I am going there to prepare a place for you' (John 14:1-3). His promise is sure; we may depend on it.

> How firm a foundation, you saints of the Lord,
> Is laid for your faith in his excellent Word!
> What more can he say than to you he has said
> You who unto Jesus for refuge have fled?

But sadly, many Christians are not aware of the adequate and trustworthy basis for their security which the Bible provides. As a direct consequence, they fail to appreciate what is rightfully theirs — like homeless people searching for a place of their own, and all the time not knowing that they are holding the title deeds to a substantial property which is rightfully theirs.

There are two main reasons for this failure to know what security the Bible promises. The first is that many Christians are not serious Bible readers. The Holy Spirit doesn't teach them because they don't open his book. The second reason is that many listen to the ministry of pastors and teachers who do not themselves seriously study and explain the Word of God in their preaching, either because they do not believe it or because they too are not aware of its importance. Some 'preachers' regard the Bible as having little relevance for today. They think the events it records are not relevant now, or even that they are fictitious. It is, they think, the word of human writers (which it is) but not the Word of God (which it also is!). Others give to the Bible superficial respect, but tend to set it on one side because they believe they have more direct and more exciting revelations from God.

Such ministers as these do not understand what it means to build the church on the foundation of the apostles and prophets (Ephesians 2:20). The sad result is that the people in their congregations have little confidence in God's Word because the man in the pulpit doesn't have that confidence either and — unlike the Bereans (Acts 17:11) — they do not examine the Scriptures for themselves to see if what they are told is true.

No-one denies that there are questions about the Bible we cannot answer but that is not a reason for ignoring it. There are many things in life we do not fully understand but we cannot afford to ignore them. (I have some difficulty in fully understanding many things in life but I know I shall be the loser if I ignore them.) How strange it would be if we did not find some difficulties in a book, written over a period of a thousand years by many different writers, who were recording truths which God has revealed about his eternal purposes! Even the prophets themselves who spoke of the grace that was to come to us 'searched intently and with the greatest care, trying to find out the time and circumstances to which the Spirit of Christ in them was pointing when he predicted the sufferings of Christ and the glories that would follow.' And 'even angels long to look into these things' (1 Peter 1:10-12).

What Jesus and the apostles taught about the Bible is far more important for us than what its critics say about it. Speaking at different times, in different places and circumstances, they agree that the Scriptures are the Word of God. 'The Scripture cannot be broken' Jesus said (John 10:35); it is 'easier for heaven and earth to disappear than for the least stroke of a pen to drop out of the Law' (Luke 16:17). Jesus used the Scriptures (in his case the Old Testament) as a powerful weapon against Satan (Matthew 4:4-10); he used them to settle controversies (Mark 12:24) and questions about morality (Matthew 19:1-9). The apostle Paul regarded all Scripture as 'God-breathed' (2 Timothy 3:16,17), and the apostle Peter insisted that 'no prophecy of Scripture came about by the prophet's own interpretation ... but men spoke from God as they were carried along by the Holy Spirit' (2 Peter 1:20, 21).

The New Testament writers also claimed God's authority for their own writings, as well as for those of the Old Testament. Peter had no hesitation in saying that the command of our Lord and Saviour was given through the apostles (2 Peter 3: 2). Paul claims that the word of the apostles is actually the Word of God (1 Thessalonians 2:13). Indeed, he invokes a curse on all who preach a gospel other than the one he preaches (Galatians 1:8). John insisted that anyone who does not agree with his teaching is not to be welcomed into the fellowship (2 John 10). The verdict of the psalmist is a fine summary of the attitude of Scripture to itself: 'Your word, O LORD, is eternal; it stands firm in the heavens' (Psalm 119:89).

In addition, we believe the Bible is God's Word because God has given us the faith to believe it and the Holy Spirit has enlightened our minds by it. We insist that all who 'do not speak according to this word' have no understanding of spiritual things (Isaiah 8:20). We believe the Bible contains 'all things necessary to salvation; so that whatsoever is not read therein, nor may be proved thereby, is not to be required of any man, that it should be believed as an article of the Faith, or be thought requisite or necessary to salvation' (Article 6 of the Church of England).

The insecure believer should know this — the knowledge which will cure his or her unhappy condition is to be found in the pages of the Bible and nowhere else. Uncertainty will continue as long as the Holy Scripture is ignored or its truth and reliability are doubted.

God's covenant

When Tom and Mary were being married, they stood side by side in church and the minister asked: 'Tom, will you take Mary to be your wife? Will you love her, comfort her, honour and protect her, and forsaking all others, be faithful to her as long as you both shall live?' Tom answered, 'I will.' Then Mary made her promises to Tom. They were entering into a covenant — a binding agreement which involved obligations and privileges for them both.

In the Bible, marriage is used as an illustration of the covenant God has made with his people (Jeremiah 3:14; Isaiah 54:5). But unlike the covenant made between Tom and Mary, which may fail because either of them may fail to keep their promises, God's covenant with his people cannot break down because his promises are sure. He has promised that believers shall be his people and he will be their God; that he will give them 'singleness of heart and action,' so that they will always fear him (Jeremiah 32:38,39). God's covenant relies upon his undeserved mercy and faithfulness toward us. This is why it is called the Covenant of Grace, for undeserved mercy is an act of grace. And there's another difference—the covenant between Tom and Mary will end when one of them dies, but God's covenant with his people goes on forever (Isaiah 55:3).

Many Christians think the Old Testament (or, the first Covenant) is all about law (God being strict) and the New Testament (or, the New Covenant) is all about grace (God being loving). They are under the impression that God introduced the New Testament because he had changed his mind about the Old. A regular member of my congregation once accused me of preaching 'too much about the cruel God of the Old Testament and not enough about the loving God of the New'!

This is a serious mistake which strikes at the very foundation of our assurance. God does not change his mind. The covenant of grace does not begin with the coming of Jesus. Indeed, we get the first hint of it immediately after the fall of Adam (Genesis 3:15) and it was firmly established with Abraham. In Genesis chapter twelve we are told that God chose Abraham and made promises to him. In chapter fifteen God called him into a covenant relationship (Genesis 15:1-18) and in chapter seventeen God confirmed that covenant: 'The Lord appeared to Abraham and said, "I am God Almighty, walk before me and be blameless. I will confirm my covenant with you ... I have made you the father of many nations ... I will establish my covenant as an everlasting covenant between me and you and your descendants after you for the generations to come, to be your God and the God of your descendants after you" ' (Genesis 17).

The covenant of grace is simply the outworking of God's eternal plan of salvation. Long before the universe was made, God the Father promised to give to his beloved Son a people for his inheritance, and he, for his part, would come into the world to redeem them (Revelation 5:9). This is very clear in the prayer Jesus prayed: 'Father, I want those you have given me to be with me where I am, and to see my glory' (John 17:6,20,24). Bishop Ryle's comments are eloquent: 'All true believers, who really repent, and believe, and have the Spirit, may fairly take comfort in the thought, that they were known and cared for and given to Christ by an eternal covenant, long before they knew Christ or cared for him' (Expository Thoughts on John p.201).

To whom then are the covenant promises made? Who are the true descendants of Abraham? Many of the Jews, his natural children, rejected their Messiah, even though they received circumcision (the outward sign of belonging to the covenant), together with all its external privileges (Romans 9:4,5). As the apostle Paul says, 'A man is not a Jew if he is only one outwardly, nor is circumcision merely outward and physical. No, a man is a Jew if he is one inwardly; and circumcision is circumcision of the heart ...' (Romans 2:28,29).

The true descendants of Abraham are those, from every nation under heaven, who follow Abraham's example of faith, as Paul explains: 'Understand then, that those who believe are the children of Abraham. The Scripture foresaw that God would justify the Gentiles by faith, and announced the gospel in advance to Abraham: "All nations will be blessed through you." So those who have faith are blessed along with Abraham, the man of faith' (Galatians 3:7-9). 'If you belong to Christ, then you are Abraham's seed, and heirs according to the promise' (Galatians 3:29).

The covenant of grace contrasts sharply with the covenant God made with Adam. To inherit eternal life under this latter covenant, Adam had to give perfect obedience to the will of God (Genesis 2:16,17) which he failed to do. It was based on the principle, 'do this and you shall live.' This is why it is sometimes called the covenant of works (i.e. deeds.) The penalty of death for Adam's trespass has fallen on the human race, for 'sin entered the world through one man, and death through sin' (Romans 5:12). But under the covenant of grace, eternal life is freely given to all who believe, because of the perfect obedience to God's law of Jesus Christ on their behalf. 'The gift is not like the trespass. For if the many died by the trespass of the one man, how much more did God's grace and the gift that came by the grace of the one man, Jesus Christ, overflow to the many!' (Romans 5:15).

The covenant of grace also contrasts sharply with the false idea that we can be right with God by obeying the commandments given to Moses (Romans10:5-10). This false idea was prevalent in Paul's day among the Jews (Galatians 3:10-14) and is still prevalent today. But when God made the covenant with Moses, he did not cancel his covenant with Abraham. Indeed, God told Moses that whenever the disobedient people of Israel repented of their sins, he would remember his covenant made with Abraham (Leviticus 26:42; Deuteronomy 4:31). God answered the prayers of Moses on the same basis (Exodus 32:13). The law was given to Moses to show how holy God is and how serious sin is (Romans 3:20) and why we need Christ (Galatians 3: 24). 'The law was added,' says Paul, 'so that the trespass might increase. But where sin increased, grace increased all the more, so that just as sin reigned in death, so also grace might reign through righteousness to bring eternal life through Jesus Christ our Lord' (Romans 5: 20,21).

So we see believers, in both Old and New Testament times, basing their assurance on the covenant of grace. At the end of his life, King David of Israel said, 'Is not my house right with God? Has he not made with me an everlasting covenant, arranged and secured in every part?' (2 Samuel 23:5). And we Gentile Christians, living at the dawn of the twenty-first century, may base our assurance on the same everlasting covenant also. We are not people of God's second thoughts; we are part of his everlasting covenant. God has committed himself to us and has promised to write his law on our hearts, to forgive our wickedness and remember our sins no more (Jeremiah 31:33,34).

Today, very many believers know nothing about the covenant of grace. It is seldom mentioned by many preachers. And most of those who have heard of it totally fail to understand its significance. Can there be any wonder they feel insecure when such a large part of the foundation truth is missing, on which their assurance must be based?

God's oath

God has gone even further to strengthen our assurance. He has confirmed his covenant promises by an oath. God's promise is sufficient in itself, of course, but he gives us even greater security by adding to it his oath. When people give evidence in many courts, they have to swear by Almighty God that they will tell the truth, the whole truth, and nothing but the truth. 'Men swear by someone greater than themselves, and the oath confirms what is said and puts an end to all argument' (Hebrews 6:16). (Lying under oath is a very serious matter). But 'when God made his promise to Abraham, since there was no-one greater for him to swear by, he swore by himself, saying, "I will surely bless you and give you many descendants"' (Hebrews 6: 13,14). 'Because God wanted to make his purpose very clear to the heirs of what was promised, he confirmed it with an oath. God did this so that, by two unchangeable things' (i.e. his promise and his oath) 'in which it is impossible for God to lie, we who have fled to take hold of the hope offered to us may be greatly encouraged' (Hebrews 6:17,18). What a gracious God we have!

God's verdict

'Who will bring any charge against those whom God has chosen? It is God who justifies. Who is he that condemns?' (Romans 8:33,34). No accusation can ever stand against us because the highest authority in the universe has pronounced us not guilty. The slate is wiped clean.

I was once in trouble with the police for parking my car without leaving the lights on. The chief constable, in reply to my letter of apology, explained that he would not take the matter any further, but that if I should offend again, my former offence would be taken into consideration. It is not like that with God. When he acquits me, all my transgressions are removed from the record for ever.

But will God now not punish the guilty, as he has always said he would? (Exodus 34:7). The fact is he does not contradict himself. The punishment for our transgression has been taken by our Lord Jesus Christ (Isaiah 53:5) so that God is both 'faithful' (to his promises) and 'just' (according to his law) 'and will forgive our sins' (1 John 1:9).

This means that one of the main causes of our insecurity — the fear of our sins still needing to be judged — may be banished forever. Even our secret sins, which have caused us so much anxiety, are now removed—if we repent of them. Their memory may now be put to better use — to help us in our continual attitude of repentance.

But knowing that 'there is now no condemnation for those who are in Christ Jesus' (Romans 8:1) does not, as some suggest, give us freedom to live as we like. On the contrary, such gracious forgiveness is a great incentive to holy living. Knowing we are justified before God creates within us a strong desire to live for his glory. Paul puts it this way: 'Shall we go on sinning, so that grace may increase? By no means! We died to sin; how can we live in it any longer?' (Romans 6:1,2).

The positive side of our justification is just as thrilling. God not only takes away the guilt of our sins but gives us the righteousness of Christ. Our transgressions are reckoned as Christ's and his perfect righteousness is reckoned as ours. We have no righteousness of our own because we have not kept God's law, but God's gift of righteousness does not depend on our law-keeping. Christ's perfect obedience satisfied the demands of God's law on our behalf. God now looks upon us as being 'in Christ.' 'No-one will be declared righteous in his sight by observing the law; rather through the law we become conscious of sin. But now a righteousness from God, apart from law, has been made known ...' (Romans 3:20,21). What firmer ground for Christian assurance can there be?

'Therefore, since we have been justified through faith, we have peace with God through our Lord Jesus Christ ... and we rejoice in the hope of the glory of God' (Romans 5: 1, 2).

God's nature

Mary's marriage to Tom, mentioned earlier, isn't going very well. She can't get the idea out of her head that Tom is unreliable. She is agitated because she thinks there's a side to his nature she doesn't yet know about. When she gets up in the morning she wonders ... is this going to be the day she makes that dreadful discovery that her husband is not to be trusted? In fact, she has no real reason for thinking this way; so the problem is in her thoughts and not in real facts.

How different our relationship with God should be! We have no need to fear that he will prove unreliable. The very thought is abhorrent. God never changes (Malachi 3:6). He is the same yesterday and today and forever (Hebrews 13:8). He loves us with an everlasting love (Jeremiah 31:3). He will always remain faithful to what he has said, for 'God is not a man, that he should lie, nor a son of man, that he should change his mind. Does he speak and then not act? Does he promise and not fulfil?' (Numbers 23:19). We may hold 'unswervingly to the hope we profess, for he who promised is faithful' (Hebrews 10:23). He who began a good work in us 'will carry it on to completion until the day of Jesus Christ' (Philippians 1:6). 'Every good and perfect gift is from above, coming down from the Father of the heavenly lights, who does not change like shifting shadows' (James 1:17). The light from the sun, the moon and the stars is always changing, but God never changes. The world he has created will perish but God remains the same (Psalm 102:26). His love is constant; his truth is constant; his will is constant.

The fulfilment of a promise depends on the character and ability of the person who makes it. People often promise more than they can deliver. They either deliberately go back on their word or find they are unable to do what they promised. But God guarantees our security because he is not only faithful to his Word, but is also able to do what he promises. Nothing is too hard for the Lord (2 Timothy 1:12).

God's choice

'Praise be to the God and Father of our Lord Jesus Christ, who has blessed us in the heavenly realms with every spiritual blessing in Christ. For he chose us in him before the creation of the world to be holy and blameless in his sight. In love he predestined us to be adopted as his sons through Jesus Christ, in accordance with his pleasure and will' (Ephesians 1:3-5). 'The godly consideration of Predestination, and our Election in Christ, is full of sweet, pleasant, and unspeakable (i.e. inexpressible) comfort to godly persons, and such as feel in themselves the working of the Spirit of Christ ...' (Article 17 of the Church of England).

Christians who deny this glorious truth forfeit their assurance. They deprive themselves of that pleasant and inexpressible comfort. And those who misunderstand the doctrine by saying that the 'foreknowledge of God' merely means that God saw in advance who would themselves decide to believe are wrong. 'The foreknowledge of God' means that all who believe were loved and chosen by God before time began, and they believe for that reason. They were appointed for eternal life (Acts 13:48). Jesus himself was handed over to be crucified 'by God's set purpose and foreknowledge' (Acts 2:23). How ridiculous it would be to suggest that God merely saw in advance that his own beloved Son would decide to perish on a Roman cross!

The teaching of Jesus on the subject is very clear: 'All that the Father gives me will come to me ... and this is the will of him who sent me, that I shall lose none of all that he has given me, but raise them up at the last day' (John 6: 37, 39).

We are fully aware of the intellectual problems this truth of election raises but we believe what the Bible teaches, not because we can fathom it but because God has revealed it. If we reject the profound revelations of God just because we cannot understand them fully, using our limited human reason, we also reject the need for faith.

The purpose of God's choice of his people is also clearly revealed. God intends to make them like Jesus. What a prospect! The apostle Paul says, 'those God foreknew he also predestined to be conformed to the likeness of his Son' (Romans 8: 29). God 'has saved us and called us to a holy life — not because of anything we have done but because of his own purpose and grace. This grace was given to us before the beginning of time ...' (2 Timothy 1:9). 'From the beginning God chose you to be saved through the sanctifying work of the Spirit and through belief in the truth' ...   (2 Thessalonians 2:13). The apostle Peter says, 'we have been chosen according to the foreknowledge of God the Father ... for obedience to Jesus Christ' (1 Peter 1:2).

So our God has determined that all whom he has chosen will be glorified and no power in heaven or on earth can prevent that. For this is the glorious plan of salvation, beginning in the eternal purpose of God and ending in the eternal glory of every believer. 'Those he predestined, he also called; those he called, he also justified; those he justified, he also glorified' (Romans 8:30). Why should any believer feel insecure?

God's gift

A tale is told about a wealthy art collector who didn't know how wealthy he was. He heard about a painting of great value and decided his collection would never be complete without it. He determined to purchase it at any price. There was only one problem — he didn't know where it was being kept. He called his assistant and told him to go and search for the treasure. Some months later his assistant returned, having travelled round the world. 'Have you found it?' the art collector asked eagerly. 'Yes' replied the assistant. 'Where?' asked the collector. 'In your own collection', the assistant replied.

In our quest for assurance it is easy to make the same mistake. We search for that something extra without realising that we possess it all the time. There are always people around who will tell us about the one thing we still need to make our joy complete. The Christians in Colosse had this problem and Paul had to remind them that they had been given 'fulness in Christ'(Colossians 2:9,10). Having 'received Christ Jesus as Lord,' Paul tells them that their duty now is to 'continue to live in him, rooted and built up in him, strengthened in the faith as you were taught, and overflowing with thankfulness' (Colossians 2:6,7) and not to go searching for something else to make them feel sure about their security as believers.

Jesus brings to all God's children everything they will need for a healthy Christian life. It is absurd to suggest that God, having given us his Son, then holds something back from us. 'He who did not spare his own Son, but gave him up for us all — how will he not also, along with him, graciously give us all things?' (Romans 8: 32). The gift of faith (Ephesians 2:8), the gift of the Holy Spirit (1 John 4:13), and the gift of eternal life (1 John 5:11) are gifts that cannot be separated from the gift of Jesus. 'All things are yours,' says Paul, '... and you are of Christ, and Christ is of God' (1 Corinthians 3:22,23). True, some of God's gifts are not yet fully appreciated by us but they are all ours in Christ. A man who inherits vast treasure may have little idea of the value of his inheritance, but it is certainly all his.

Since the gift of Jesus is the greatest expression of God's love, what else do we need to be sure of eternal life? Jesus is now our brother and we are co-heirs with him. What the Father gives to his Son, is therefore shared by all his people. What he inherits, we inherit.

God's seal

Every true Christian without exception has received the gift of the Holy Spirit. It is not possible to be a Christian otherwise. Without the Spirit no-one can say (from the heart) 'Jesus is Lord' (1 Corinthians 12:3). 'We were all baptized by one Spirit into one body' (1 Corinthians 12:13).

The indwelling Spirit acts as a seal. 'Having believed,' says Paul, 'you were marked in him with a seal, the promised Holy Spirit' (Ephesians 1:13). Seals are used on legal documents to prove their authenticity. They are used on containers as a safeguard against pilfering. In the past, a person would put his private seal on documents instead of signing them. He would use his seal to mark and protect his personal property. The seal was a mark of genuineness, identification, and a security against theft. True believers are sealed by the Holy Spirit for all these reasons. The Spirit in believers confirms their genuineness. They have this testimony in their hearts (1 John 5:10). He has 'set his seal of ownership upon us' (2 Corinthians 1:22), and he ensures that we are kept securely (Ephesians 4:30).

The apostle Paul also speaks of the Spirit as a deposit. The Spirit, he says, is a deposit guaranteeing our inheritance. A deposit is a first instalment that gives an intending buyer a legal right to the goods. It is a pledge that guarantees what is to come (2 Corinthians 5:5). By giving us the Spirit as a deposit,

How can I be sure?

God ensures that we are his everlasting possession, one day to
enjoy the fulness of what that means.

Key points of chapter seven — the means of assurance

- fulfil the conditions
- examine ourselves
- trust in the Lord
- know your inheritance
- live holy lives
- make every effort
- use the means

7.
The means of assurance

Fulfil the conditions

There are no special conditions to be fulfilled by us in order to
qualify for God's promises of salvation. Our eternal security
depends on God's decree and power and not on anything we
do. 'For it is by grace you have been saved' says Paul, 'through
faith — and *this not from yourselves*, it is the gift of God'
(Ephesians 2:8). God has blotted out our transgressions for his
own sake (Isaiah 43:25); he has qualified us 'to share in the
inheritance of the saints' (Colossians 1:12).

But the promises of *assurance* do have conditions attached
to them. Being sure of our salvation *does* depend to some extent
on what we do. The apostle John is very clear about this: 'We
know that we have come to know him if we obey his commands'
(1 John 2:3) 'If anyone obeys his word, God's love is truly
made complete in him. This is how we know we are in him:
Whoever claims to live in him must walk as Jesus did' (1 John
2:5,6). 'Dear children, let us not love with words or tongue but
with actions and in truth. This then is how we know that we

belong to the truth, and how to set our hearts at rest in his presence' (1 John 3:18,19).

Are not these conditions impossible for us to fulfil? How can we possibly reach such a high standard? We need not be alarmed — John is not saying that the only way to be sure of our salvation is to be perfect. If this were the case there would be no such thing as assurance for anyone! What John is telling us is that the more we grow in obedience, the greater our sense of security will be. After all, confession of our sins is itself a matter of obedience (1 John 1:9) and we shall never reach the point in this life where we have no sins to confess.

On the contrary, as we grow in grace we will become more aware of our sins because we become more aware of God's holiness. The gap between his standards and ours seems to grow wider because, as we grow in grace, we have clearer views of his perfection and more honesty about our own shortcomings. 'If we claim to be without sin,' says John, 'we deceive ourselves and the truth is not in us' (1 John 1:8). Believers who feel sure of their salvation cannot be guilty of such self-deception because where there is no contrition, there can be no assurance (Psalm 51:17). Those who claim to be without sin know nothing about the grace of God.

Here then is a paradox — obedience that leads to righteousness (Romans 6:16) is a condition of assurance, but feeling satisfied with any rightness we have attained is a barrier to being sure! Going forward continually to greater attainments is the only safeguard against insecurity. As Paul puts it, 'Not that I ... have already been made perfect, but I press on to take hold of that for which Christ Jesus took hold of me' (Philippians 3:12).

We have to come to realise the fact that the Christian life will be a fight against sin until the day we die. The struggle to rid our minds of impure thoughts will be constant and unrelenting. This is because as believers we now disapprove of our own sinful thoughts and actions. 'The sinful nature' says

Paul, 'desires what is contrary to the Spirit, and the Spirit what is contrary to the sinful nature. They are in conflict with each other, so that you do not do what you want' (Galatians 5:17). Whenever I have been asked to counsel believers who were alarmed by their own sinfulness, I have always found that it had not occurred to them that their new consciousness of sin was itself a sign of grace.

This makes daily repentance a paramount condition of assurance. Many Christians feel insecure simply because they do not have contrite hearts. In fact, their failure to see the need for daily repentance is an enormous barrier to their progress in the faith. Perhaps they have been neglecting the means of grace but will not admit it. Perhaps they love a particular sin and are making excuses to justify their doing it. Or perhaps they are blaming others, blaming their circumstances, or even blaming God for their failures. Those who persist in these attitudes will find that the joy of forgiveness will be displaced by hardness of heart and a bitterness of spirit that will seriously hinder their growth in assurance. Or perhaps they have made repentance difficult because they are filled with remorse over a serious moral lapse of some kind and cannot forgive themselves. Being unaware of the wretchedness of their sinful nature (Romans 7:14-25) and of the boundless mercy of God (Micah 7:18), they find it hard to believe that a child of God could be guilty of such a thing, or that he or she may be freely forgiven, whatever the sin, if there is true repentance.

Whatever the cause, Christians who are reluctant to repent make themselves feel insecure. They should learn that where sin is concerned, frank confession is the only way forward. They should know that God's grace is never exhausted. They should realise that their stubbornness will stand between them and the joy of salvation until the matter is put right (Psalm 51). They may not be able to do anything about the scars caused by their sins, but they can certainly do something about the uncertainty their sins may cause.

But the repentance must be genuine. It must be accompanied by fervent prayer for cleansing, for inner purity, for strength to conquer sin. It must bring with it a determination to be more disciplined in the use of the means of grace.

The enjoyment of assurance then, depends to a large extent on what we do. But that does not make it something we earn. Assurance is God's precious gift to his children, based on the same trustworthy nature of God as the gospel itself, and is conveyed to our hearts by the Holy Spirit. But like many of God's gifts, it cannot be enjoyed by those who persist in disobedience and refuse to repent. If we fail to use the means for our security which God has provided and do not 'live as children of light' (Ephesians 5:8) we are guilty of grieving the Spirit and we must not expect him to give us assurance in our disobedience.

Examine yourselves

If we feel insecure, the cause must be found. To do this, we must ask ourselves some basic questions. Have we fully understood what God has done for us in Christ? Do we know what it means to be justified by faith? Have we been neglecting the means of grace — study of the Bible, worship, Christian fellowship or prayer? Have we believed anything without checking it carefully against the Word of God? Is there some sin we are unwilling to confess and forsake? Are we blaming God for some apparent tragedy in our lives?

Examining ourselves simply means comparing our beliefs and behaviour with the teaching of Holy Scripture. Everything we need, in order to test ourselves, will be found there (Isaiah 8:20). Our Christian friends may be a good example to us, but we must be very careful about judging ourselves by the standards of others. They too may be failing in some way and may lead us astray (Galatians 6:4). The Bible is the only safe guide.

How can I be sure?

I remember hearing Bishop Festo Kivengere of Uganda tell the story about a farmer teaching one of his labourers how to plough a straight furrow. 'Keep your eye fixed on some object at the far side of the field,' the farmer said, 'and then go straight for it.' Some time later the farmer returned to find the furrows were anything but straight. 'Why didn't you take my advice?' the farmer demanded. 'I did,' the labourer replied, 'I kept my eye on that cow over there.' No doubt the cow moved!

It is not easy to make a true assessment of our spiritual progress. Our personal character all too easily affects our thinking. If we have a tendency to think of ourselves as full of faults, we may be easily discouraged. In that case, we should remember that we have a God who loves us freely and is ready to heal our waywardness (Hosea 14:4). 'A bruised reed he will not break and a smouldering wick he will not snuff out' (Isaiah 42:3). If we have the opposite tendency and cannot readily see our failings or find it hard to admit them, we may easily deceive ourselves and imagine all is well when it is not. In this case, we should ask God for the ability to see ourselves in a true light and for the humility and courage to face up to what we see. He will help us make a true assessment of ourselves if we are serious about it.

The need for balance in self-examination is important. It is just as foolish to spend too much time examining ourselves as it is to spend too little. Introverted believers may think so much about their own spiritual problems that they fail to show any concern for the problems of others. Extroverted believers on the other hand can just as easily think so little about their own spiritual health that they are hardly aware of their shortcomings. And all of us, whatever our characters, can be guilty of seeing the failings of other believers more readily than we see our own. We do, of course, have a responsibility towards fellow-believers, but we do not serve their interests, nor indeed our own, if we do not deal first with our own failings. The plank in our own eye will prevent us from seeing clearly enough to remove the speck from our brother's eye (Matthew 7:5).

I had a friend who used to do all his own car servicing and repairs and was never happy driving it if the servicing was overdue or if it had developed a fault. Indeed, he was so keen to keep the car in perfect condition, that it was frequently off the road because it was in pieces. The car was not a lot of use to him. I have another friend who never looks at the engine of the car. He just puts petrol in the tank and drives about. As one would expect, the car breaks down frequently, and the cost of repairs tends to be high. We must avoid spending too much, or too little time in examining our spiritual life, to see if it is healthy.

Remember too, it is our spiritual health today we must assess, not yesterday's. The victories of the past should be an encouragement to us, but we must not be content with past victories alone. It is no use trying to conceal the defeats of the present with the victories of the past. Christians who have retired from daily work need to be watchful at this point. Having retired from work it is easy to think we have retired from the spiritual battle as well. It is important to remember our adversary never retires. Age and experience do not provide exemption from daily spiritual warfare (Ephesians 6:11).

Trust in the Lord

Before Mary was married to Tom (see page 44), she believed him to be trustworthy. At that point she was free to keep that belief to herself and not commit herself to him. But it was a very different matter once she had accepted Tom's proposal of marriage. Now she had to put her belief into action; she had to put her trust in him, because her future happiness now depended on his trustworthiness.

Faith is much more than an intellectual acceptance of the fact that God is trustworthy. We may believe this very sincerely in our minds and yet never enter into a practical relationship with him. Having faith in God means actually putting our trust in him. It means committing our lives to him for ever. It means, as far as our salvation is concerned, we are relying on nothing else and on no-one else.

The Bible makes it clear that faith includes trust. Indeed, the words 'believe' and 'trust' are sometimes linked together in such a way that they mean the same thing. For example, in the Psalms we are told that disobedient Israel 'did not believe in God or trust in his deliverance' (Psalm 78:22). The Psalmist is not saying two different things, but the same thing in two different ways. Believing in God is trusting in his deliverance. When the disciples of Jesus did not trust in him, he rebuked them for their lack of faith (Matthew 6:30; 8:26). So to be lacking in faith means to be lacking in trust.

Again, when we are told that 'Abraham believed the LORD' (Genesis 15:6), it means he acted on what God said. He went forward in faith, relying upon God to do what he had promised. So says the writer to the Hebrews: 'By faith Abraham, even though he was past age — and Sarah herself was barren — was enabled to become a father because he considered him (God) faithful who had made the promise' (Hebrews 11: 8,11).

The same writer tells us that Abraham, along with the other patriarchs, lived 'by faith.' They 'were still living by faith when they died. They did not receive the things promised; they only saw them from a distance' (Hebrews 11:13). They are described as men of faith because, in spite of all the contrary evidence, they trusted what God said. (We now have all the more reason to trust God, since Christ has come, lived, died and rose again, as an historical fact.)

It is this 'trust' element in faith which gives assurance. 'They who trust in the LORD are like Mount Zion, which cannot be shaken but endures for ever' (Psalm 125:1). Obviously, if our trust is complete, our assurance will be complete as well.

But if we feel insecure because our faith is small, we must do what the apostles did and ask God to increase it (Luke 17:5). We must make use of the means God has made available to us, just as they did. He has given us 'everything we need for life and godliness through our knowledge of him who called us by his own glory and goodness' (2 Peter 1:3).

Know your inheritance

All the riches of our eternal inheritance are ours if Jesus is ours. In Christ we have everything. God has already 'blessed us in the heavenly realms with every spiritual blessing in Christ' (Ephesians 1:3). He has 'raised us up with Christ and seated us with him in the heavenly realms' (Ephesians 2:6). Our assurance grows, not because our inheritance grows but because our understanding of our inheritance grows. The fact is, we are all, spiritually, far richer than we think and we must go on diligently studying the Bible to discover how rich we really are (Colossians 1:27).

In spite of these plain truths, the wicked suggestion is often heard that it is possible to be a believer without being in full possession of all that God gives in Christ. Such an idea is one of Satan's foul and favourite lies and it undermines our assurance. We must not be deceived. Satan knows that if we believe that lie, we are likely to waste our time searching for something in addition to Christ, and fall prey to insecurity. The blessing of assurance is not for a favoured few who have been given something extra or have had special revelations of some kind; it is for every believer without exception. God has given 'his very great and precious promises' to every believer so that through them we may 'participate in the divine nature and escape the corruption that is in the world through evil desires' (2 Peter 1:4). Those who do not participate like that are not true Christians.

This doesn't mean that we shall not sometimes make new and exciting spiritual discoveries. On the contrary, spiritual life will be full of delightful surprises. Becoming a Christian is like inheriting a gold-mine. I have no idea how much wealth lies hidden under the surface, but I know it all belongs to me and I shall go on being surprised by the nuggets of gold I discover. All the necessary excavating equipment is at my disposal and it is now my duty and my pleasure to start digging in God's Word.

Live holy lives

Contrary to popular belief, holiness is not the rigorous imposition of a religious discipline on a reluctant human spirit —perhaps even involving withdrawal from the secular world. Holiness is Christ-like behaviour motivated by a Christ-loving heart.[1] A truly Christ-centred personal and private life is bound to show itself in a Christ-honouring public life. Conversely, religious behaviour that does not spring from a desire to please God is not Christian holiness; nor is any religious experience which does not affect my inner thoughts and motives. Holiness involves self-discipline, as we shall see shortly.

It will be clear from this that knowledge of God's revealed truth is essential to holiness, for we cannot please God if we do not know what his will is. This is why Paul describes himself as 'an apostle of Jesus Christ for ... the knowledge of the truth that leads to godliness' (Titus 1:1). In his prayer to his Father, Jesus made the same point— 'sanctify them by the truth; your word is truth' (John 17:17).

Without holiness assurance is impossible. Unless we take time to discover what the will of God is and seek his strength to obey it, we shall never escape from the crippling effects of our insecurity. The only way we may 'know that we have come to know him' says the apostle John, is to 'obey his commands' (1 John 2:3). James too, insists that the blessing of the Christian life comes not merely with knowing the Word but with doing it (James 1:25). The Holy Spirit increases our assurance by opening our minds to the truth and strengthening our wills to obey it.

In turn, as our assurance increases, so does our longing after truth and holiness. For example, an increasing awareness that we are predestined to be conformed to the likeness of God's Son (Romans 8:29) cannot but lead to an increasing eagerness to know more about Jesus and to make progress towards his glorious likeness. Why should we idly wait for the glory to come? 'When he appears' says John, 'we shall be like him, for we shall see him as he is' — and then he adds, 'everyone who has this hope in him purifies himself' (1 John 3:3). In other words, we do not wait idly for the likeness of Christ to be seen in us. According to Paul we are already being transformed into the Lord's likeness 'with ever increasing glory' (2 Corinthians 3: 18).

Some have argued that assurance has the opposite effect and can make us careless about spiritual things. What incentive to live a holy life can there be, they ask, if we know in advance that we are going to heaven? But these objectors are wrong. What they say is clearly contrary to the teaching of Scripture and also to Christian experience. The Bible gives no encouragement to those who think they can continue in sin here and now and go to heaven hereafter (Romans 6:1,15), and no believer has ever known the joy of assurance without also hungering and thirsting after righteousness (Matthew 5:6). To know that God has chosen us, inevitably creates within us a strong desire to please him (Colossians 3:12).

Holiness is an essential preparation for heaven for all believers. It is not an additional blessing for a favoured few. Everyone whom God calls out of darkness is at the same time called to holiness. We are to be holy because he who called us is holy (1 Peter 1:14,15). 'It is God's will for you' says Paul, 'that you should be holy' (1 Thessalonians 4:3). God chose us 'to be saved *through* the sanctifying work of the Spirit' (2 Thessalonians 2:13) which means we are to be made holy in this world as a preparation for the next. None enter heaven except those who are made holy *before* they go there. 'Without holiness no-one will see the Lord' (Hebrews 12:14).

101

This does not mean that we have to be without sin before we can enter heaven. The fact is, the attainment of sinless perfection must wait *until* we enter. One of the essential features of true holiness is a godly discontentment with our present attainments. Christians who are satisfied with their progress are not making any! But discontentment is not a sign of insecurity. Those who rejoice in the knowledge that their destiny is to be like Jesus, can never be content with their spiritual growth.

If we are determined to grow in holiness we shall have a hard task these days. We shall not only have to face hostility from the world, which has always felt threatened by godly people, but we may also have to cope with hindrances in the church, in which little or no teaching is given on the subject. Many church-goers, and perhaps even members of our own family, will disapprove. Not knowing the difference between true holiness and what is considered to be acceptable social behaviour, they will say we are being extreme. To make progress in holiness in these circumstances two things are vital—regular and careful study of God's Word, and a persevering and prayerful resolve to be obedient to it (2 Timothy 3:16).

A word of warning may be necessary here. Since it is God's purpose that all whom he calls will be made holy, those who show no evidence of willingness to make progress in the Christian life cannot safely assume that they are children of God. Holiness is the indispensable evidence of our election (Ephesians 1:4).

Make every effort

Although it is God who makes us holy (1 Thessalonians 5:23), growth in holiness is not achieved without effort on our part. This is stressed throughout the New Testament. 'We must pay more careful attention to what we have heard ... so that we do not drift away' (Hebrews 2:1). We must 'throw off everything that hinders and the sin that so easily entangles' and 'run with perseverance the race marked out for us' (Hebrews 12:1). We must overcome evil with good (Romans 12:21). We must 'make every effort to do what leads to peace and mutual edification' (Romans 14:19).

Wherever we look in the New Testament we find the same practical emphasis. We are to control our tongues (James 3:9-12), to respect our wives (1 Peter 3:7), to honour our parents (Ephesians 6:1,2), to bring up our children in the training and instruction of the Lord (Ephesians 6:4), to look to the interests of others (Philippians 2:4), to live, as much as possible, at peace with everyone (Romans 12:18). We are to say 'no' to ungodliness and worldly passions, to live self-controlled, upright and godly lives (Titus 2:12), to offer our bodies as living sacrifices to God and not to conform any longer to the pattern of this world (Romans 12:2). We are to let the Word of Christ dwell in us richly (Colossians 3:16), devote ourselves to prayer (Colossians 4: 2), and do everything for the glory of God (1 Corinthians 10:31). All this demands effort.

The need for effort in our private devotional lives is also stressed. We are to watch and pray to avoid temptation (Mark 13:38). We are to set our hearts and minds on things above and not on earthly things (Colossians 3:1,2). We are to think about the things that are true, noble, right, pure, lovely and admirable (Philippians 4:8). We are to have our minds set on what the Spirit desires (Romans 8:5). We are to strive to keep our consciences clear before God and other people (Acts 24:16).

If we respond whole heartedly to these New Testament demands, we shall be rewarded with increasing confidence. The apostle Peter tells us that it is by making every effort to add these Christian qualities to our faith that we make sure of our calling and election (2 Peter 1:5-11). It is the sluggard who 'craves and gets nothing, but the desires of the diligent are fully satisfied' (Proverbs 13:4). 'Blessed are they who keep his statutes and seek him with all their heart' (Psalm 119:2).

'God is not unjust;' says the writer to the Hebrews, 'he will not forget your work and the love you have shown him as you have helped his people and continue to help them. We want each of you to show this same diligence to the very end, *in order to make your hope sure*. We do not want you to become lazy, but to imitate those who through faith and patience inherit what has been promised' (Hebrews 6:10-12). 'The effect of righteousness will be quietness and confidence for ever' (Isaiah 32:17). 'Those who have served well gain an excellent standing and great assurance in their faith in Christ Jesus' (1 Timothy 3:13).

If we would only make more effort to live holy lives, to keep up a daily habit of communion with our Lord; if only we would try harder to 'grasp how wide and long and high and deep is the love of Christ' (Ephesians 3:18) and to work out our salvation 'with fear and trembling' (Philippians 2:12) we would be pleasantly surprised at the new spiritual discoveries we would make, the new joys we would experience, and how much more secure we would feel.

When I was quite a young Christian, I was taught by some well-meaning but misguided believers that emphasis on the need for our efforts in this matter dishonours the Spirit, and that faith provides an easier way. Accepting the teaching without question, I very quickly became disillusioned and, if wiser counsel had not prevailed, I think I would have found myself in spiritual difficulties for years. Of course, these teachers were partly right because we cannot achieve anything by our own unaided effort. Without the help of the Spirit we are helpless, and without faith we cannot please God (Hebrews 11:6). But this 'let go and let God' idea, as it is sometimes called, is not found in Scripture. It is a serious error to think that having the Spirit relieves us of the need for effort, or that faith offers a short cut to holiness. The duty of putting to death the misdeeds of the body rests squarely on our shoulders and when we take it seriously, the Spirit helps us (Romans 8:13). We shall never reach the point in this life beyond which we cannot make progress and therefore, whatever degree of assurance we may have attained, we must not relax our efforts for a moment.

In summary, our growth 'in the grace and knowledge of our Lord and Saviour Jesus Christ' (2 Peter 3:18) — so essential to our growth in assurance — is not achieved without sustained effort by us.

Use the means

We have already seen that one of the causes of spiritual insecurity is the neglect of the means of grace. Therefore it is vital that we diligently use whatever means God makes available to help us spiritually. Half-heartedness in this matter will simply not do.

The early Christians 'devoted themselves to the apostles' teaching and to the fellowship, to the breaking of bread and to prayer (Acts 2:42). They were eager to learn together, eager to love one another, eager to remember the death of their Master together, and eager to pray together. With such dedication, their growth in assurance was guaranteed.

Their example is a model for us. We can't attend the apostles' teaching sessions as they did, but this is no disadvantage. Their teaching is recorded faithfully in the New Testament, so that we too may benefit. 'The full riches of complete understanding' (Colossians 2:2) were not just for the early church.

In view of the unthinking way in which the words 'teaching' 'fellowship' 'worship' and 'prayer' are often used, it is important to understand their biblical meaning. The word 'fellowship' for example, is often used for what is no more than idle conversation. The participants may be talking about football, a programme on TV, their aches and pains or the weather. Not that there is any harm in that, but it is not fellowship in the strict sense. 'Fellowship' means encouraging one another in the Christian life — considering how to 'spur one another on towards love and good deeds' (Hebrews 10:24,25). 'Teaching' is the giving of instruction in apostolic truth. 'Worship' is the glad response of our minds and hearts to God's truth and love. 'Prayer' is our natural and necessary response to our heavenly Father's revelation — he speaks to us through his Word by his Spirit and we answer in prayer. It is the means whereby we thank him for his goodness, claim his promises, seek his grace, and tell him all about our needs.

Teaching, fellowship, worship and prayer are interdependent activities. Teaching is essential to fellowship (Colossians 3:16), to worship (John 4:24) and to prayer (1 John 5:14). Fellowship is the context in which teaching, worship and prayer take place (Ephesians 5:19,20). The Bible knows nothing about God's people deliberately worshipping in isolation as a regular practice. The idea of 'going to church' without hearing the Word preached, or 'having fellowship' without an opportunity to pray together and encourage one another, would have been unthinkable to the early Christians.

Private Bible-study and prayer are also essential to our growth in assurance. Praying in private is not just an opportunity for telling God about the problems we cannot mention in public. It is a means whereby we may know God better. As God speaks to us through his Word, and as we respond to him in our prayers, we grow in understanding. Diligence here is very important for believers who find themselves in churches where the worship is shallow, the teaching poor and the fellowship almost non-existent. Because there is nowhere else to go, many Christians find themselves in this situation and worshipping somewhere is better than worshipping nowhere. In their private devotions they should make every effort to make good what they miss in public worship.

The discipline of private prayer is not easy. Finding the time for it proves difficult for many believers and finding the words to say is difficult for all. But the Spirit 'helps us in our weakness' and 'intercedes for us with groans that words cannot express' (Romans 8:26). Words are always inadequate anyway, because no believer can properly understand the deep spiritual longings of their hearts. But the Spirit of God understands those longings perfectly because he put them there. 'He who searches our hearts knows the mind of the Spirit, because the Spirit intercedes for the saints in accordance with God's will' (Romans 8:27). What a comfort it is to know that the Spirit interprets, censors, amends and supplements our prayers, so that we are protected from the consequences of our own ignorance. We should lose a lot in our lives if God only answered our prayers just the way we uttered them!

But this is not a prescription for laziness. We don't just leave the Spirit to translate our sighing and groaning. Jesus promised to do whatever we ask in his name, 'so that the Son may bring glory to the Father' (John 14;13). This puts us under an obligation to search out God's will from God's Word and be as precise as we can in our prayers. God is glorified in our asking even if we don't get it exactly right. And the knowledge of past mistakes must not deter us from fresh effort. 'Let us approach the throne of grace with confidence, so that we may receive mercy and find grace to help us in our time of need' (Hebrews 4:16).

(1)   Readers may like to know of the title *Aspects of holiness* published by Grace Publications, ISBN 0946462 55 0, which gives a full study of the subject of the biblical teaching about holiness.

Key points of chapter eight — the blessings of assurance

- patience
- contentment
- humility
- courage
- consistency
- usefulness
- joy
- thankfulness
- peace

8.
The blessings of assurance

When I was learning to swim I had to start in the shallow end of the pool. I remember it was always rather crowded at that end and I had some difficulty weaving my way across the pool from side to side. Stubbing my toes or banging my knees on the bottom added to my problems. What a joy it was to take to the deeper water. Of course, the water is just the same at both ends — but there's more of it at the deep end.

So it is with the blessing of assurance, which is not a different sort of blessing from the other blessings of the Christian life — the only difference is in its intensity. Every believer should experience the joy of the Lord in some measure, but the *fulness* of joy is reserved for those who feel confident to take to the 'deeper water' of growing spiritually. Every believer should have patience, contentment, consistency, humility and courage to some extent; but these blessings will be *more* evident in the lives of those who feel sure about their spiritual position. All believers should be of some use in the service of Christ but with assured hearts their usefulness will be greatly *increased*. Every believer should have a spirit of thankfulness, but those who are secure will have more occasion for praise — praise that is not generated by particular circumstances, but springs spontaneously from the heart in all circumstances.

Patience

The day is surely coming when Christ 'will transform our lowly bodies so that they will be like his glorious body' (Philippians 3:21). God will wipe every tear from our eyes and 'there will be no more death or mourning or crying or pain' (Revelation 21:1-4). Death will be 'swallowed up in victory' (1 Corinthians 15:54). What a glorious prospect! In the meantime however, we 'groan inwardly' (Romans 8:23) because we find it hard to maintain our spirituality under the pressures of our sinfulness and mortality.

To have the patience we so much need under this constant pressure, a confident expectation of the glory to come is essential. Without that we shall not easily avoid the unworthy reaction of worry and bitterness. 'We wait eagerly' says Paul 'for ... the redemption of our bodies' and 'if we hope for what we do not yet have, we wait for it patiently' (Romans 8:23-25). As our hope grows stronger, so will the patience.

Jesus himself is our great example here. The writer to the Hebrews tells us to 'fix our eyes on Jesus' and 'run with perseverance the race marked out for us' because he too was greatly encouraged in his hour of trial by the prospect of future glory. 'For the joy set before him' he 'endured the cross, scorning its shame, and sat down at the right hand of the throne of God' (Hebrews 12:2).

But it is not only the confident expectation of future glory that gives us patience; it is also the sure knowledge that our heavenly Father has a purpose in all our sufferings in the meantime. Persecution, sickness, 'accidents' and bereavements will be borne without a murmur when we are persuaded that God uses them all for good, even though we may not understand how this may be. This assurance will save us from the folly of

111

blaming God for laying burdens on us which (we say) are too heavy to carry. We know that whatever happens to us, our times are in his hands (Psalm 31:15) and 'if the earthly tent we live in is destroyed, we have a building from God, an eternal house in heaven, not built by human hands' (2 Corinthians 5:1).

As well as telling us to follow the example of Jesus, the writer to the Hebrews also tells us to 'imitate those who through faith and patience inherit what has been promised' (Hebrews 6:12). He links faith with patience in this way to teach us that faith works by giving us patience to wait for the inheritance God has promised. During the waiting period, faith accepts (passively) with fortitude what God permits, and pursues (actively) with perseverance what God promises. This means that our growth in fortitude and perseverance will depend to a great extent on the increase and activity of our faith.

As we said earlier, being sure of God's overruling providence does not mean being immune from trouble. Indeed, it sets us free from the idea that Christ will solve all our problems, heal all our diseases and turn life into one long pleasant experience — an idea which has brought disillusionment to many people. Secure believers are realists; they do not expect God to give them preferential treatment in this world. On the contrary, because their aim is to do the will of God, they will expect — in an ungodly world — to meet more trials and tribulations, not less, and will suffer patiently because they know that not even a hair of their heads can be lost without God's consent (Matthew 10:30).

The anguished question — 'What have I done to deserve this?' will never cross their minds. Instead, they will say with the Psalmist, 'A righteous man may have many troubles, but the LORD delivers him from them all' (Psalm 34:19) and 'I will lie down to sleep in peace, for you alone, O Lord, make me dwell in safety' (Psalm 4:8). They will be happy in the knowledge that every trial will end as soon as their heavenly Father's purpose is accomplished. In the meantime, instead of seeing trials as tokens of divine disfavour, assured believers will learn to use them as the means by which faith is increased.

Contentment

With patience comes contentment, for if our hearts are overflowing with joy because of the treasure we know we have in heaven, there will be no room for dissatisfaction with our lot in life. And if we are convinced of the dependability of God's promises of protection, we will not fret about our circumstances.

In particular, we will be free from the impoverishing and distracting desire for riches. 'Keep your lives free from the love of money and be content with what you have,' says the writer to the Hebrews, 'because God has said, "Never will I leave you; never will I forsake you." So we say with confidence, "The Lord is my helper; I will not be afraid. What can man do to me?"' (Hebrews 13:5, 6). The apostle Paul too was talking about money when he said: 'Godliness with contentment is great gain' and 'people who want to get rich fall into temptation and a trap and into many foolish and harmful desires that plunge men into ruin and destruction' (1 Timothy 6:6-10).

This contentment co-exists quite happily with that godly restlessness about our spiritual attainments that we were talking about earlier. Godly contentment is not complacency. We are not relieved of the responsibility to strive after holiness — which, incidentally, includes the good stewardship of our money and the care of our health — but we are relieved of the vanity and futility of thinking we can always control our circumstances. We are liberated from the folly of believing that if only things were different we would be far better Christians — if we lived somewhere else, had a different job, or a different marriage partner. Instead, we shall patiently 'submit to the Father of our spirits and live!' (Hebrews 12:9). We shall know the secret of being content in any and every situation ...' (Philippians 4:11,12). We shall be willing to humble ourselves before the Lord, knowing that he will lift us up (James 4:10).

113

Humility

The virtue of humility, some argue, is not attainable by those who claim to be sure about going to heaven. Assurance creates pride, they say, and makes us self-satisfied. If we want to be truly humble we must be uncertain. Only then shall we be saved from complacency and spurred on to greater effort. But nothing could be further from the truth. True humility, like assurance itself, rests on the knowledge that we were chosen in Christ 'before the creation of the world' (Ephesians 1:4) and that Christ has done everything to secure our salvation. We are saved by grace (Ephesians 2:8). Being assured of these things makes us realise that we do not we deserve, and cannot merit, even the least of God's mercies. That ensures that we are kept humble, and that is a great blessing.

Those who cling to the idea that eternal life is attained by their own efforts are exposed to the sin of pride. The confident believer will always echo the words of Paul — 'By the grace of God I am what I am, and his grace to me was not without effect' (1 Corinthians 15:10), and 'May I never boast except in the cross of our Lord Jesus Christ, through which the world has been crucified to me, and I to the world' (Galatians 6:14). Boasting in anything else other than what Christ has done betrays our lack of assurance. Without his grace we are poor lost sinners.

Courage

Believers who confidently expect to receive 'the crown of righteousness' (2 Timothy 4:7,8) and who take hold of the eternal life to which they are called, will be blessed with courage to fight the good fight of faith (1 Timothy 6:12). The fear of men, that causes so many believers to cower before a hostile world and hide their lamps under a bowl (Matthew 5:15), will be banished from their hearts.

'I eagerly expect and hope that I will in no way be ashamed, but will have sufficient courage so that now as always Christ will be exalted in my body, whether by life or by death. For to me, to live is Christ and to die is gain' (Philippians 1:20,21). These words of Paul, written in prison, clearly show that it was his firm assurance of eternal life that gave him the courage to speak out for Christ. They also show that the possibility of denying his Lord, perhaps in the hope of obtaining release, never came into his mind because he knew that the question as to whether he would be released or executed would be decided by a higher authority than that of the Roman emperor. Whether he lived or died, he knew he was safe in the hands of his God.

The same principle holds good for us, even though we may not be called on to suffer like Paul. When we are tempted to deny the Lord because of what people may say or do to us, our confidence in God's gracious promises and in his overruling providence will give us sufficient courage to exalt Christ whatever the cost. We are on the victory side and we know that others can only do to us what God permits.

Consistency

As we grow stronger in the faith we will be blessed with greater consistency in our beliefs and behaviour (Colossians 2:6,7) — no longer 'tossed back and forth by the waves, and blown here and there by every wind of teaching' (Ephesians 4:13,14), and no longer growing tired of 'doing what is right' (2 Thessalonians 3:13). Instead, we will be 'established and firm, not moved from the hope held out in the gospel' (Colossians 1:23), and we shall persist in doing good (Romans 2:7).

Our behaviour will be more consistent because we will be free from the instability of double-mindedness (James 1:8) and free from the notion that God may have deserted us when life is difficult. We will serve the Lord with greater faithfulness (Joshua 24:14), with that rare quality of reliability (which will safeguard us against beginning confidently and then losing heart) and with a keener awareness of our duty to God (which will give us a greater sensitivity about conduct that is not in keeping with our duty).

Being consistent in our beliefs and behaviour doesn't mean we shall close our minds or 'despise the LORD'S discipline' (Proverbs 3:11). On the contrary, we will be constantly checking our beliefs by Scripture teaching and making adjustments where necessary (a habit we must develop if we are to grow in confidence) and we will always be ready to acknowledge our shortcomings.

Usefulness

'Whoever believes in me,' Jesus said, '... streams of living water will flow from within him' (John 7:38). This teaches us that Jesus not only fully satisfies the hearts of believers but makes them overflow so that others are blessed through them. We simply cannot deny that the feeble faith of many Christians, and the poor witness which results from that, severely limits the fulfilment of this glorious promise.

An old English hymn conveys the thought of Jesus' words: 'He will never disappoint you! Jesus is far more to me than in all my glowing daydreams I had fancied he could be; and the more I get to know him, so the more I find him true, and the more I long that others should be led to know him too'.

Believers who feel secure in the love of God will be motivated by a strong desire to live a useful life. The question, 'How can I repay the Lord for all his goodness to me?' (Psalm 116:12) will always be in their minds. No longer crippled by anxiety about their salvation, or about the Lord's promises, they will be free to give their minds to the serious business of serving the Lord. So it was with the apostle Paul. 'We are confident ...' he says, 'and would prefer to be away from the body and at home with the Lord. So we make it our goal to please him ...' (2 Corinthians 5:8,9).

116

Every believer is called to witness. 'Always be prepared' says the apostle Peter, '... to give the reason for the hope that you have' (1 Peter 3:15). 'You are a chosen people, a royal priesthood, a holy nation, a people belonging to God, that you may declare the praises of him who called you out of darkness into his wonderful light' (1 Peter 2:9). The stronger our hope so the greater will be our preparedness to give the reason for it; the more convinced we are of being 'a people belonging to God' so the more emphatic will be our witness in praise of him.

Can anyone deny that many Christians are uncertain and therefore bring only a half-hearted commitment to Christian service? The need for Christians who are sure of their faith and eager to give themselves fully to the tough task of serving the Lord in today's world, has never been more urgent. There is no task more fulfilling than this and those who serve well have no regrets in old age. At the end of a life of faithful service, the apostle Paul was able to say, 'I have fought the good fight, I have finished the race, I have kept the faith. Now there is in store for me the crown of righteousness, which the Lord, the righteous judge, will award me on that day - and not only to me, but also to all who have longed for his appearing' (2 Timothy 4:7,8).

The privilege of serving the Lord is a great blessing and every believer is called to serve. But how much greater the blessing when we are able to serve with deep conviction!

Joy

What the apostle Peter calls 'an inexpressible and glorious joy' should be the experience of all to whom God has given new birth (1 Peter 1:3,8). Why then do so many believers fail to discover it? Is it not because of their insecurity? Their uncertainty inhibits their rejoicing.

The Scriptures clearly teach that the gospel is a cause for great rejoicing. The birth of our Saviour is 'good news of great joy' (Luke 2:10,11). The kingdom of God to which we belong, is a matter of joy in the Holy Spirit (Romans 14:17). Jesus taught his disciples that through their loving obedience, his joy would be made complete in them (John 15:11). 'Rejoice in the Lord always,' says Paul, 'I will say it again: Rejoice!' (Philippians 4:4).

The Scriptures also tell us that our heavenly Father rejoices over us because we are now part of his family (Luke 15:23,24). The Lord Jesus rejoices over us because we are the fruit of his sacrifice (Isaiah 53:10-12; Hebrews 12:2). 'There is rejoicing in the presence of the angels of God over one sinner who repents' (Luke 15:10). What a sad thing it is if we, who are the cause of all this rejoicing in heaven, are so uncertain about our own position that we cannot join in that joy.

Christian joy relates to the forgiveness of sins (Matthew 9:2). The deeper our assurance of forgiveness is, the greater will be our joy. Joy also comes from our expectation of future glory — the more confident we are that our 'names are written in heaven' the greater will be our rejoicing (Luke 10:20). (Clearly, our ability to rejoice 'in the hope of the glory of God' is determined by the strength of that hope Romans 5:2). Joy also springs from our conviction that God is able to keep us from falling and to present us 'before his glorious presence without fault and with great joy' (Jude 24). The more convinced we are of his keeping us, the greater our joy will be in the meantime. Joy grows from faith and the fulness of joy springs from the fulness of faith. Paul made this clear when he told the Philippians that he would continue working for their 'progress and joy in the faith' (Philippians 1:25).

For years after Mary married Tom (Chapter 6, p. 79) she was still not happy. Her doubts about Tom's faithfulness persisted and, to make matters worse, she knew in her heart that she had not felt able to trust him completely from the start of their marriage — a fact which Tom had not failed to notice. With this at the back of her mind all the time, Mary did not find much joy in their relationship. It was all the more sad because her doubts and fears were without foundation.

If we feel insecure in our relationship with God, whether our uncertainty arises from doubts about his faithfulness or from our own inability to trust him wholly, how can we rejoice? Uncertainty about important matters always has a tendency to generate anxiety, and nothing is more important than the matter of our eternal destiny. We need to realise that our doubts and fears are without foundation. 'God is not a man that he should lie, nor a son of man that he should change his mind. Does he speak and then not act? Does he promise and not fulfil?' (Numbers 23:19).

Contrary to popular belief, assurance also helps us enjoy the pleasures of this life more than unbelievers can. A sure hope of glory gives a totally new meaning to this life and enables us to keep it in its proper perspective. Our appreciation of all the good things God richly provides 'for our enjoyment' (1 Timothy 6:17) is heightened, and our ability to avoid the pleasures of sin, which bring so much sorrow, is increased (1 John 3:3).

From time to time the Lord may lead us through dark and lonely valleys and we will be downcast (Psalm 42:5), but even in these circumstances we shall be able to rejoice because we know that 'our present sufferings are not worth comparing with the glory that will be revealed in us' (Romans 8:18). In the light of that glory, our present troubles will never get out of proportion. 'Though outwardly we are wasting away,' says Paul, 'yet inwardly we are being renewed day by day. For our light and momentary troubles are achieving for us an eternal glory that far outweighs them all' (2 Corinthians 4:16,17). We are 'sorrowful, yet always rejoicing' (2 Corinthians 6: 10).

Thankfulness

An assured heart is always a thankful heart, a heart set free from the anxiety of uncertainty about this life and the next and therefore freed from all those worries which inhibit praise. We shall be free from the fear of men and 'say with confidence, ' "The Lord is my helper; I will not be afraid" ' (Hebrews 13:6). We will be free from the insatiable desire for pleasure, possessions and high position in society (1 John 2:16) that makes people so miserable and so ungrateful; from that spirit of bitterness about their sufferings that often gives vent to blaming God instead of praising him. We shall be free from the desire for revenge against those who hurt us (Romans 12:19,20)— a desire that so effectively stifles praise and thanksgiving. In its place we shall have a forgiving spirit that praises God, bears insults, and endures trials.

The great outbursts of praise in the letters of Peter and Paul demonstrate these truths vividly. So sure are they of God's salvation and so full of gratitude, there is no room for grumbling (Philippians 2:14) or bitterness (Ephesians 4:31). Their praise flows like a river in flood. 'Praise be to the God and Father of our Lord Jesus Christ, who has blessed us in the heavenly realms with every spiritual blessing in Christ. For he chose us in him before the creation of the world to be holy and blameless in his sight. In love he predestined us to be adopted as his sons through Jesus Christ, in accordance with his pleasure and will ... In him we have redemption through his blood, the forgiveness of sins, in accordance with the riches of God's grace that he lavished on us ...' (Ephesians 1:3-14). 'Praise be to the God and Father of our Lord Jesus Christ! In his great mercy he has given us new birth into a living hope through the resurrection of Jesus Christ from the dead, and into an inheritance that can never perish, spoil or fade ...' (1 Peter 1:3,4).

Peace

All who are justified by faith are at peace with God in the sense that God is no longer angry with them. They are 'reconciled to him through the death of his Son' (Romans 5:10). But awareness of this new situation varies from believer to believer according to the degree of their assurance. The more satisfied we are that God no longer counts our sins against us (2 Corinthians 5:19) the less our consciences will accuse us. The more we are assured of our new status, the less we shall be in fear of God's wrath (Romans 1:18;5:1). Peace in our minds and hearts rests on the firm assurance that Christ has paid the debt of our sin and secured our pardon.

The sure knowledge that God is in complete control of the circumstances and events of our lives also gives us peace (Romans 8:28). Such knowledge guards our hearts and minds with the peace of God 'which transcends all understanding' (Philippians 4:6,7). We no longer live in fear of things going wrong. We are happy to echo the words of the Psalmist: 'Lord, you have assigned me my portion and my cup; you have made my lot secure' (Psalm 16:5).

The link between the assurance of faith and inner peace is well established in the Bible. 'You will keep in perfect peace him whose mind is steadfast' said Isaiah, 'because he trusts in you' (Isaiah 26:3). 'Do not let your hearts be troubled,' Jesus said, 'Trust in God; trust also in me' (John 14:1). 'Peace I leave with you; my peace I give to you ... Do not let your hearts be troubled and do not be afraid' (John 14:27). Paul makes the same connection: 'May the God of hope fill you with all joy and peace as you trust in him ...' (Romans 15:13).

Poor Mary, of whom we spoke earlier; for years she had been filling every waking moment with frenzied activity so that she would not have too much time to think about her unhappy marriage. But things are changing! She is discovering at long last that her fears about Tom not being trustworthy are without foundation. The marriage is secure after all! The doubts were all in her own mind. What's more, she has asked Tom's forgiveness for her failure to trust him — a request which he granted without the slightest hesitation. These days, after the children have been put to bed, she loves to sit and chat with her husband and no longer feels ill at ease in his company. But why did it take her so long to trust Tom?

To have a mind at peace — no longer disturbed by continual doubts about the permanence of our relationship with God; no longer to be troubled by an uneasy conscience or crippled by anxiety about the future, is one of God's richest blessings for his people. Our forgiving God (Psalm 130:4) is utterly trustworthy and we are his for ever. 'The LORD blesses his people with peace' (Psalm 29:11); having that assurance, we need not doubt any longer.

Postscript

1 Corinthians 11:27

A friend of mine has just told me the sad story of a lady who refused to take the bread and wine in the communion service. She gave two reasons — first, that she was 'not worthy' to do so and, second, that she had not had 'a word from the Lord' to say that she was one of his elect.

In all probability, the lady was familiar with the Authorised Version of 1 Corinthians 11:27: 'Whosoever shall eat of this bread, and drink this cup of the Lord *unworthily*, shall be guilty of the body and blood of the Lord', and she had completely misunderstood it. The error is not uncommon.

The early church observed the Lord's Supper in a very different way from us. Christians met to eat a meal together, probably bringing their own food with them and, after they had eaten, they would remember the Lord's death, using the bread and wine left over from the meal. It was known as the 'love-feast' (Jude 12). In Corinth, however, greed and drunkenness had turned the observance into a disgraceful scramble. The abuses were so serious that the apostle Paul found it necessary to tell them that it was not the Lord's Supper at all (1 Corinthians 11:20), and that by behaving in this *unworthy manner*, they were 'guilty of sinning against the body and blood of the Lord.' If the lady, and others like her, had consulted the later versions of the Bible, she would have known that this was Paul's meaning, for they all render *unworthily* by the words *unworthy manner*.

To think that *anyone* could be a worthy communicant in his or her own right is a serious mistake. Christ died, 'the righteous for the unrighteous' (1 Peter 3:18); that is to say, the worthy for the unworthy. In the communion service, we remember his body broken for us, and his blood poured out 'for the remission of sins' (Matthew 26:26-28). How, then, can anyone be a worthy participant?

However, there is a sense in which we are made worthy through Christ, and in all the places where the New Testament speaks of people being worthy to enter the kingdom of God (Luke 20:35; 2 Thessalonians 1:5, etc.), this is what is meant. It is one of the glories of the gospel that Christ takes helpless and hell-deserving sinners and makes them fit for heaven. It is his merit, not ours, which makes us worthy. In this sense, therefore, and only in this sense, may we speak of being worthy participants in the communion service. What a pity the lady did not understand this.

Her second reason was even more misguided. After all that the Lord has done to guarantee the salvation of his people, and to make them feel secure, this lady still thinks he has not done enough. If she really believes that God reveals the way of salvation in his Word, and confirms its truth to our hearts by his Spirit; if she is aware that along with new life in Christ, God gives us the spirit of sonship so that we may know he is our Father; if she is conscious of the fact that he enables us by his Spirit to live holy lives so that we may have the evidence within us that we are God's children, and if she knows he has provided the means of grace so that our assurance may grow stronger, how can she possibly feel the need of a further word from the Lord? Christians can only feel this need because they either do not, or will not, spend time listening to God speaking through his Word.

God does not regard his written Word as inadequate (2 Timothy 3:15). There is therefore no need for God to speak directly to this lady. Why should he give to all believers a solid basis for assurance in his Word, and then grant additional assurance to one individual independently of it? And if in these circumstances she were to receive what she believed to be 'a word from the Lord', the danger of self-deception would be very great.

All through the history of the church, people have claimed to receive messages from God. I can think of several such people during my own ministry, some of whom even claimed divine sanction for doing the most bizarre and immoral things. We should not be surprised at this because 'Satan himself masquerades as an angel of light' (2 Corinthians 11:13-15). I do not suggest they were knowingly making false claims. In some cases they had obviously mistaken their own strong emotions for the voice of God, and their subsequent actions exposed the hollowness of their claims.

None of this must be taken to imply that God does not guide his children in the many choices and decisions they have to make in those areas where the Bible cannot be specific — questions like, 'What vocation shall I choose?', 'Who shall I marry?', 'Where shall I live?' But these are very different matters. They involve much prayer and patience, a willingness to consult other mature believers and the ability to think biblically. And, in fact, the Bible does give more guiding principles on such matters than many Christians realise. There is no need for 'special' words from the Lord when guiding principles are already in his written Word!